"Out of the pain of his own life, Alton Beech offers hope, encouragement and insight to those who are struggling. This book will be a lifeline in a time of storm."

—JAMES ROBISON
FOUNDER AND PRESIDENT
LIFE OUTREACH INTERNATIONAL
FORT WORTH, TX

"This book should be read by every Christian who has found it difficult to press beyond the pain of past hurts, failures and disappointments. This timely word can be the midwife that encourages you to push beyond the pain ... forgetting those things which are behind ... and give birth to destiny and purpose."

—BISHOP GEORGE G. BLOOMER
SENIOR PASTOR
BETHEL FAMILY WORSHIP CENTER
DURHAM, NC

push

Push Beyond Your Pain

How to Survive Your Wilderness Experience

A. J. Beech

CREATION
HOUSE
PRESS

Push Beyond Your Pain by A. J. Beech
Published by Creation House Press
A part of Strang Communications Company
600 Rinehart Road
Lake Mary, Florida 32746
www.creationhouse.com

Unless otherwise noted, all Scripture quotations are from
the King James Version of the Bible.

Library of Congress Catalog Card Number: 2001090383
International Standard Book Number: 0-88419-786-7

01 02 03 04   5 4 3 2 1
Printed in the United States of America

Acknowledgments

First of all, I would like to thank my Lord and Savior, Jesus Christ, for making this book possible. As with everything in my life, this book was inspired by the experiences of my own life.

I want to thank the apple of my eye, my lovely wife, Tina Beech, for her support in finishing this work. Her input, editing and encouragement were invaluable. I also want to thank my kids, Nyeisha, Taychon, Rachel and Elijah for their love and support; and the Greater Anointing Harvest Church family for supporting me in my endeavors.

I would also like to thank Brother Laurence Johnson and Mr. and Mrs. Donald and Ana Boyd. Special thanks to Minister Marvena Graham for editing.

Dedication

This book is dedicated to my wife, Tina, and our four children, Nyeisha, Taychon, Rachel and Elijah; to the Greater Anointing Harvest Church; and also to all the poor and hungry people throughout the world.

Contents

Preface

Don't be surprised if you begin to see yourself reflected in these pages. It is sure to happen, because the issues discussed in this book are universally relevant. My hope is that the turning of these pages will bring a life-changing experience to your circumstances.

I would also like to offer another word of encouragement to you, the reader. Do you feel the calling to write a book, or do some other work for the glory of God, but continue to lay aside the opportunity to do so? If so, I call unto you right now to recognize the greatness that God has placed within you; I beseech you to stir up that gift He has given you so that you may richly bless others.

Introduction

Before you read this book, you need to know that whatever circumstance or problem you are facing in your life, it isn't too difficult for God. No matter what it is, He can handle it! He still works miracles! He has worked miracles in my life, and He will also work miracles in *your* life!

Let me tell you a little about my background. I got my first job in 1985, at the age of 17. But, within a year-and-a-half, I changed jobs about a dozen times. I finally realized that I was having trouble holding down a permanent job.

Meanwhile, I met a friend, and we became best buddies. One day my friend suggested that we quit our jobs and begin selling drugs. At that time, making $4 per hour, it sounded like a good idea. But, of course, I did not know what the outcome would be. We had only $30 between us, so we searched for a dealer who was willing to sell us enough drugs to get started. With that first supply, we made $140 in profit!

Within a year, "the business" took off. I purchased cars and all kinds of things that I wanted. Then I started to support most of my family members who were in need. As I began making thousands of dollars, I was able to drive as many cars as I wanted—Volvos, Cadillacs and Mercedes. I had fifteen cars within five years!

I embraced my "success" and became the leader of my gang—traveling from state to state, living the thug life. I "spread my wings" by recording and producing my own record, and I even made a television appearance.

But I began to feel a painful emptiness in my life. In an attempt to fill the emptiness, I began spending more money on material things and surrounding myself with women. But the pain did not go away, and I just felt more and more empty.

One day, a memory came to my mind about my father before he died. I remembered when I was six or seven years old, my father would take my brothers and me to church every Sunday. I clearly remembered my father kneeling at the altar as he ate something white and drank something that I thought was tonic (I did not know that he was taking Holy Communion). That memory led to another. I began to remember how I, at twelve years of age, walked two-and-a-half miles to go to church, and then walked the same distance back home again. And then I vividly remembered a certain man from that church saying to me, "Boy I tell you, one day God is going to use you!"

Those memories inspired me to go back to church on Sunday mornings. I began dropping hundreds of dollars in the collection plate just to get some peace of mind. But it didn't work.

I began reading my Bible. I was most interested in the Book of Psalms, but my main motive was to seek God's protection. I started reading like never before, yet I continued living the same reckless life. However, my circumstances began to change, and it seemed like everything I tried no longer succeeded.

Just when I thought my life couldn't get any worse, it did. Another friend approached me and asked me why I was buying drugs when I could get them for free. I asked how I could get free drugs, since a kilo of cocaine cost thirty-five to forty thousand dollars. He suggested that instead of paying for the kilo, I should steal it. At the time, his suggestion made sense, so I did it.

I became like Robin Hood—stealing from the rich (drug dealers) and giving to the "needy." I was putting my life in danger, not only for money, but for a new thrill. Suddenly, I was wanted by the drug dealers! I became very fearful and confused. I had seen many of my friends lose their lives playing this game, so I felt death knocking at my door. I wanted it all to stop, but the situation was out of control, and it only got worse. As my life spiraled deeper and deeper into darkness, I put the lives of everyone around me in danger. Bullets began flying through the streets, and kids had to run for their lives... all because I had ripped-off drug dealers.

Then I began watching Christian television programs on TBN (Trinity Broadcasting Network). I also found myself doing something very strange—I began praying before going out to commit my crimes. It sounds crazy, but it's true!

One day my born-again twin brother invited me and my friends over to his house to pray for us. So I went with the intention of getting prayer for divine protection for one of my crime sprees. As we began to pray, my brother anointed me with oil, and something strange began to happen. I felt like I was spinning, and my mouth began to speak a language that I had never heard. I could not understand what I was saying, and I knew that something powerful was in control of my mind, my mouth and my body. I wanted to ask my brother what was going on, but I couldn't, because my mouth was too busy speaking the new language. I did not understand what had happened, and my brother did not explain anything to me.

After that experience, I tried to continue my life of crime. But in the midst of doing wrong, I would hear a voice speak to me and tell me not to do it. I tried to ignore the voice, but it wouldn't go away. I began to hate the things I was doing.

God continued chipping away at my hard heart! I found myself doing something very bizarre. I began sharing the gospel with those to whom I was selling drugs. I could not keep my mouth shut. I became known as the "Christian drug seller." I would get very angry when people called me a Christian drug seller, and I would tell them that I wasn't a Christian. But I could not stop talking about Jesus. I tried to figure out how to stop talking about Jesus, but the more I sold the drugs, the more I would talk about Him. And it was ruining my drug business!

Other bizarre things began to happen. Many of my associates ended up going to jail, but not me. People began to think that I was an informant, because every time I would leave a scene, the cops would show up. I didn't realize that God was trying to get me to surrender my life to Him by protecting me from going to jail.

He even used a dog to save me from jail. One night I was standing on the corner with over one thousand dollars worth of drugs in my hand. That particular night, I was by myself. But there was a dog in the neighborhood that I did not like, and that dog showed up unexpectedly at the same time the police showed up. In a panic, I dropped the drugs at my feet. I knew I was caught red-handed. The officers handcuffed me and put me in the car. Then they began to search for the drugs, but they could not find them! I sat in the car wondering why the police couldn't find the drugs. They had no choice but to let me go with a warning. When I began to search for the drugs myself, I realized what had happened. The dog had picked up the drugs and carried them away.

Yet still, I couldn't see God's hand protecting me, and I continued running from Him. Amazingly, all during that time, the Lord used me to speak prophetically to people. Many of the people with whom I shared the gospel ended up dead a week or two or even months later. Even my closest friend got shot and died. I was supposed to be with him the night he was killed, but a small voice told me not to go around him. Afterward, when I asked the Lord if my friend was in heaven or hell, I saw a vision of my best friend in the torments of hell. I knew I was being warned.

Then one day my brother left a gospel tape in my car. At the time, I was listening to a rap tape with lyrics about sex, drugs and death. But a small voice told me to listen to the gospel tape, and so I did. The gospel lyrics spoke to me so clearly. It was like the Lord Himself speaking directly to me. He told me about "a man who was searching for me . . . a stranger from Galilee . . . And when I heard it was Jesus with a gift for me . . . He said, 'Meet Me on Calvary.'"

It was a simple but supernatural moment. I suddenly knew I had to stop running. Finally, after watching everything around me become chaotic and confused, I kept hearing a voice in my mind telling me to surrender my life to Jesus, or else I would die like my friends. Remembering the vow I made to God, I asked Him to kill me if I did not surrender my life at a certain time. I also asked Him one more time to show me if He was really real.

On a Thursday night, I prayed before I went to sleep. Later that night, as unbelievable as it sounds, I saw a Bible floating in mid air! But I was still not convinced, so the following night, I prayed the same prayer. That night I got what I was looking for. I fell asleep on my back, then I got up. But strangely, my body was still lying on the bed with my spirit standing on the outside. Then I saw the devil as if he were coming to get me, but he turned and left through the closed door. Then, somehow, I got back into my body. The next morning, I was terrified! I was immediately led to a church, where I met with the pastor and was baptized. I have been serving God ever since!

Part I

Push Beyond Your Pain

Talking about pain is a very delicate subject. In fact, because we are creatures with emotions, many of us may try to shy away from the subject. However, refusing to face our pain will continue to create repercussions until they are dealt with. We must remember that God created us and blessed us with emotional feelings. Yes, we were blessed when we were born with feelings. However, we must also keep in mind that manipulation of our feelings is one of the enemy's strategies to cause us to not function the way we should. Past hurt—things from which we have not been healed—is one of the enemy's avenues for playing with our feelings.

That is why I always encourage those whom I counsel to make sure they deal with the past hurt and put aside that which is irrelevant. I stress how important it is for each of us to go back to those deep places and confront the things we do not want to face. Facing and dealing with the pain now is so very important; because if we do so, then we can go forward in our lives, no longer paralyzed by the pain.

We have all been hurt through many different ways. In some cases, it has been through lack of knowledge, At other times, we have been hurt by people we trusted—maybe by our own brothers and sisters in the church, or even church leaders. Oftentimes, people have not meant to hurt us or may not have even known they have done so. Many times, people unintentionally do and say things that wound us, but their lack of knowledge and understanding causes them to see their actions as being harmless.

This is why young converts (who are usually so full of zeal, but often lack wisdom) need the right mentors to speak into their lives and give them special guidance. If you are a young convert (God bless you), be sure to ask your pastor or another church leader to help you find the right mentor. A mentor's guidance and your obedience to the Scriptures will serve to protect you. Without these two key components, you may be open for the greatest hurt of your life.

I point this out because many people's pain did not begin and end in their worldly lives, but instead they received fresh wounds after their new conversion as babes in Christ. This is one reason why our churches are filled with people who have issues with each other.

Some of this division in the church could be alleviated if we would simply spend more time getting to know each other. We would then see each other more deeply, beyond the surface of what is portrayed to the public. We would begin to see some of those deep-rooted hurts from the past that have been hidden from human eyes—that had not taken the time to look beyond the outward appearance. Understanding our own pain and the pain of others helps us to see ourselves and one another more clearly. People who avoid dealing with their pain generally tend to burden others with their own pain. Knowing this, we can now see that getting to know each other will help us to better understand and respond to the actions and reactions of our brothers and sisters in Christ.

We only need to look as far as our daily newspaper to see the extreme results of people who are tormented by their own pain. Time and time again we read about people who have become so frustrated about what has happened to them in the past that they go out and kill an innocent person who had absolutely nothing to do with the perpetrator's painful past. For example, rather than dealing with their own personal pain, child-molesters abuse others instead, and then blame their crimes on what some friend or relative did to them in the past.

Suicide is also often the result of unresolved pain. Instead of facing it head on, some people even take their own lives trying to escape the pain they once encountered and still suffer. Loners have often isolated themselves because of the pain that had once been inflicted on them. Many of them skip from church to church, or choose to stay home because they think no one could possibly understand them the way they understand themselves.

It is sad to say, but there are times when you just have to let them some of these hurting people go. In some cases, you will find that no matter what you do for them, you just can't please them or seem to make any difference whatsoever.

You can take them out to lunch, invite them over for dinner, buy them suits or dresses; but you won't be able to please them until they are willing to face the truth about themselves. You just won't be able to reach them until they are no longer blinded by their own pain.

Some of these people are so blinded they actually believe that you owe them everything in life. Then, if you are the one who is not controlled or manipulated by their sad stories and tears, they will jump to the conclusion that you don't love them. Again, they are blinded by their own pain, consumed by their own issues. They simply will not be able to see clearly until they face the truth about themselves.

Nevertheless, many people carrying around their pain do remain in the church. However, they will not be productive in the church they are presently attending, especially if they have been hurt by a member from a previous church they attended. This is because they perceive people in their new church to inflict the same pain that they felt in the church they left. Some of those people who do not face the pain they experienced in the previous church will be afraid to commit—the lack of which can ultimately cause division.

If we do not deal with our pain, the Lord's will cannot be done in our lives—no matter how many gifts we have. If a particular wound is not healed, then we will encounter trouble later on because we will run away instead of confronting that pain again. Running is not the answer to our deliverance. The answer is to confront our pain so that we can go on in life.

People who don't face the reality of the pain from their past are sometimes moody, argumentative complainers because they are held captive by their own pain.

If you are suffering in this way, you do not have to suffer

any longer. You can break that cord through the power of forgiveness by talking about it to your leader and praying for the anointing of God on that certain situation.

Let us look at the apostle Paul's life and see how he pushed beyond his pain in order to reach his goal. In Acts 14:19–20, we see that Paul went back into the city of Lystra where he had just been stoned to the brink of death. Of course, Paul did not go back to the city because he wanted more pain; but he would not allow his pain to stop him from going back there—possibly because he realized that he would never be able to go back preaching the gospel if he were to allow his pain to stop him.

In another case, in Acts 21:11–13, the Bible records how after the prophet Agabus prophesied that Paul would be bound in Jerusalem, Paul tells his brethren that he is ready to die at Jerusalem for the name of the Lord Jesus:

> And when he [Agabus] was come unto us, he took Paul's girdle, and bound his own hands and feet, and said, "Thus saith the Holy Ghost, So shall the Jews at Jerusalem bind the man that owneth this girdle, and shall deliver him into the hands of the Gentiles."
>
> And when we heard these things, both we, and they of that place, besought him not to go up to Jerusalem. Then Paul answered, "What mean ye to weep and to break mine heart? for I am ready not to be bound only,

but also to die at Jerusalem for the name of
the Lord Jesus."

Also, in 2 Corinthians 11:24–27, Paul began to
speak of the pain he experienced, and yet we know
that he stood victorious.

> Of the Jews five times received I forty
> stripes save one. Thrice I was beaten with
> rods, once was I stoned, thrice I suffered
> shipwreck, a night and a day I have been in
> the deep; In journeyings often, in perils of
> waters, in perils of robbers, in perils by mine
> own countrymen, in perils by the heathen, in
> perils in the city, in perils in the wilderness,
> in perils in the sea, in perils among false
> brethren; In weariness and painfulness, in
> watchings often, in hunger and thirst, in fast-
> ings often, in cold and nakedness.

As we read, we see that Paul dealt with a lot of
painful situations. While many other people might have
used these painful experiences as quicksand to go
deeper in despair, Paul was not conquered by the pain.
Instead, he used the pain as a springboard of strength
to go forward. He was also freed from all the pain he
had gone through.

Let us look at another example of Paul and Silas in a
painful situation.

In Acts 16, we read that even after they had been
severely whipped and thrown into a dark jail cell, Paul

and Silas still had the strength to pray and sing praises unto the Lord. Instead of complaining, Paul and Silas pressed forward.

The Bible is full of wonderful testimonies of people who suffered great pain or loss, and yet came forth triumphant in the Lord. Job is a wonderful example of one who took time to worship God even though he had many duties to attend to. (See Job 1:20.) However, his testimony does not stop there. Even after he had lost everything, he continued to speak forth the praises of God, refusing his wife's urgings for him to curse God and die. At the end of his time of suffering and loss, God gave Job twice as much as what he had before. Unlike Job and Paul and Silas, many people today say that they cannot worship God because of their pain. However, they are missing out on one of the best cures for pain—worshiping God.

Let us look at the woman with the issue of blood (Mark 5:25–34). She had been duped and hurt for twelve years. She was only met with more disappointment, suffering and loss each time she went to the people she thought would bring healing from her sickness. Did she quit? Did she give up? No, she continued to push forward in faith until she found healing.

There are many people with issues; if only they were to look for a healing, they would be made whole. In John 5:2–5, we read about a man who had been suffering with an infirmity for thirty-eight years. He was lying near the pool of Bethesda, waiting for an opportunity to be healed. However, he could not get his healing until Jesus showed up.

"When Jesus saw him lie, and knew that he had been now a long time in that case, he saith unto him, 'Wilt thou be made whole?'" (John 5:6)

Notice this, Jesus did not just ask the man if he wanted to walk again. Instead, He asked the man, "Wilt thou be made whole?"! Being made whole is much more than having the strength and ability to walk. Being made whole is the healing of the spirit, mind, soul and body!

I believe that after thirty-eight years this man's infirmity had become more than just the impotence of his flesh. His infirmity also included the impotence of his spirit and his emotions (which is the soul).

I am convinced that this man had become so aggravated and bitter in his spirit that he even began to complain in the very moment when Jesus was giving him an answer as to his healing. Instead of answering Jesus' question and saying, "Yes, I want to be made whole," the man began to describe how no one had been there to help him into the pool before someone else stepped in before he did. Jesus did not even address the man's complaint. Instead, "Jesus saith unto him, Rise, take up they bed, and walk" (John 5:8).

In whatever way you are hurting, Jesus wants to make you whole! He wants to make you whole so that you can move forward in your life.

Paul learned to push forward in his life:

> This one thing I do, forgetting those things which are behind, and reaching forth unto those things which are before, I press

toward the mark for the prize of the high
calling of God in Christ Jesus.
—PHILIPPIANS 3:13–14

And Paul says to, "Fight the good fight of faith, lay hold on eternal life, where unto thou art also called..." (1 Tim. 6:12).

Yes, push beyond that which is irrelevant and begin to think constructively—instead of destructively. With so much abundance awaiting us in Christ Jesus, why would we remain stuck with our pain—which can be healed. Philippians 4:13 states that we can do all things through Christ who strengthens us.

We must not be ignorant to the devil's trick to try to keep us living our lives around our pain, believing that we cannot be healed. The enemy uses fear as a tool to keep us from dealing with our pain. There are many people who want to be free, but the fear of dealing with their past keeps them stagnant.

Isaiah 41:10 states, "Fear thou not; for I am with thee: be not dismayed; for I am thy God: I will strengthen thee; yea, I will help thee; yea, I will uphold thee with the right hand of my righteousness."

We are not alone, and we do not have to face our pain alone. God will walk with us through our pain. In fact, many times, our pain is not as bad as we think it is. Second Timothy 1:7 says that God has not given us the spirit of fear; but of power, love and a sound mind. We must remain steadfast in the knowledge that we have the power of God to overcome, the love of God to encourage us and a sound mind to find our way out.

Proverbs 23:7 tells us that as a man thinks in his heart, so is he. Surely, that is why Philippians 4:8 encourages us to keep our thoughts aright.

Like you, I have been hurt by people in the world and in the church; sometimes people have hurt me intentionally, sometimes unintentionally. In either case, I have been able to use those painful situations to push me forward. I absolutely refused to allow those situations to keep me back.

However, before this could happen, I had to come to terms with the fact that that no one, except God, promised me anything. This realization propelled me forward so that I could overcome by forgiving those who had hurt me. I was truly able to respond in accordance with Matthew 5:44, "But I say unto you, 'Love your enemies, bless them that curse you, do good to them that hate you, and pray for them which despitefully use you, and persecute you.'"

In fact, I came to the same realization as that of Joseph, one of the great heroes of the Old Testament. Although Joseph's own brothers had plotted against him and had sold him as a slave in Egypt (where he had spent many of his years in prison), he told his brothers, ". . . Fear not: for am I in the place of God? But as for you, ye thought evil against me; but God meant it for good, to bring to pass, as it is this day, to save much people alive" (Genesis 50:19–20). Just as Joseph expressed here, I came to the realization that God was using my hurtful situations to bless me so that I could then be a blessing to other people.

Are you beginning to understand why you have to

go through what you are going through now? You can start responding—in positive and productive ways—to your circumstances, right now. At this very moment, you can get out of bed, put your phone back on the hook, pull back your shade, get yourself together and tell the devil he is a liar! Now is the time to stand up, begin to drive your fear out and walk back into your destiny.

Remember, your destiny with God is not defeat and destruction. God has a much better pathway on which you are to walk. Do not wait for your pastor to lay hands on you and speak into your life; instead begin right now to lay hands on yourself and speak words of affirmation and consolation into your own life. Shout it out! Begin to shout out where you are going; and get ready for your new beginning, a new attitude, and the spirit of David, which said, "I shall not die, but live, and declare the works of the Lord" (Ps.118:17).

My friend, do not be cast down; but instead let the sun rise up in you and conquer everything that once conquered you. No longer let your pain defeat your purpose that God has ordained for you. Do not let your pain be your guide, because if you do, it will surely lead you to settle for less.

Settling for less can take many forms. For example, some people have multiple partners because their pain takes them from one to the other. Those who are caught in this maze are trying to get fulfillment from one another; but instead they are only storing pain on top of pain. There are also many people who are like the crippled man who sat at the gate of the temple called Beautiful (Acts 3:2). Like the crippled man, they are sitting at the gate, looking for a temporary fix to an immediate problem. However, unlike the crippled man who received his healing, many people are not willing to get over the pain of being spiritually crippled. You may know someone like that, someone who tends to talk about the same old pain every time you are with them. You may even be like that yourself. You may find yourself compelled to rehearse the details of that same old pain over and over to anyone who will listen. Remember, you cannot be forced to be healed; but if you are willing, you can be made whole. In John 16:33, Jesus said that in the world you will have pain or tribulation, but you can be of good cheer because He has overcome the world and in Him, you will have peace. Yes, you can have wonderful and unspeakable peace and comfort in Him.

Do you carry a hurt so deep that the very mention of someone's name upsets, frustrates or agitates you? Certainly, living that way is not God's will for your life. Instead, God wants to heal us from every symptom of our pain. It is time to move beyond your cringing and shortness of breath when you find yourself having lunch with that ex-husband, that ex-wife, that boss, that sister or brother, that relative or those *used-to-be* friends. From this day forward, begin to use those situations as springboards to recovery. Do this by repeating to yourself, "As from this time forth, I will carry no more dead weight. I will not let my pain lead me to discouragement and defeat; I will instead use my pain as a highway to victory."

Worry is another form of pain. Many people carry a pain of wondering why they are not married or why it is taking so long for them to get married. But keep in mind that God is molding and shaping us as we go through seasons of uncertainty or hardship. We can find comfort and understanding in Romans 5:3–4, ". . . tribulation worketh patience; and patience, experience; and experience, hope."

The key word here is hope; hope that in God's time you will receive if you faint not.

On the other hand, some people who have not dealt with their past pains from their previous relationships, begin to have problems in their new marriage. This is because they have carried their old hurts into the new relationship and are often burdening their spouses with their own pain.

Other people are afraid to confront their pain from abortions they had in the past and now feel condemned by their action. Many of them try to conceal the pain but whenever the word *abortion* is mentioned, their pain resurfaces. Fortunately, by the grace of God, many have begun to realize that the only way to move beyond this pain is to confront it, be healed from the wound and go forward.

You may experience different levels of pain. One of the worst kinds of pain is when you feel like you are carrying a bowling ball in your chest. This pain seems to move up and down whenever you are confronted by a familiar situation or emotion that triggers it. It makes you silent because it feels like the pain is filling the air passage of your throat, rendering you unable talk about it. So you do what you (and so many others) do best—force it back inside of you and believe that it will just go away.

If you will admit that you are a person who is carrying any of the types of pain mentioned above, please allow me to give you a remedy:

Number 1: Start to forgive and pray for those who hurt you.

Number 2: Find someone to whom you can safely express your feelings. This person should be someone who will be understanding and non-judgmental.

Number 3: Release your tears, because shedding tears is a mechanism for releasing and healing the pain that has built up inside of you.

Number 4: Learn to be a "praiser." Praise can help heal what is inside.

Do you tend to shut down when your pain surfaces? Going into your shell is not the answer to resolving painful feelings, because when you become silent, you are suppressing the pain. The pain must be released, not buried and covered up. If not, you'll find yourself releasing your pain on your family, your coworkers and/or your church brothers and sisters.

The people who refuse to receive counsel are usually on a pathway that can lead from pain to bitterness. When ugly bitterness takes root, the people who have gone down this pathway begin to assume that everyone is their enemy. These are the people who persecute you, slander you and fight you; all because of their pain.

Suppressing or covering up pain can take many forms.

For some, it takes the shape of mistaking what "love" really means. People caught in this web wander from one relationship to another, wondering why they can't seem to be able to find the right person, not realizing that they always hook up with the wrong person because they go into the relationship for the wrong reasons.

Some use sex to cover the pain; others use drugs or alcohol to escape their pain.

Using these things to cover the pain leads to addiction, and until we stop accusing and blaming others, we will not see ourselves clearly enough to steer away from the lies that hold us in addiction. Proverbs 4:23 warns us to guard our hearts because out of it flows the issues of life. This means that we must guard our affections (or weaknesses) and other sensitive areas that are more vulnerable to the deception of the enemy.

If the enemy can get to those sensitive areas, he can destroy you and hinder you from fulfilling your purpose, just as he snares millions of people each day with his lies.

In order for us to protect something, we must first know what it is that we are securing. That is why we must stay in the Word of God, remaining steadfast in the knowledge of who we are in Him. Then, with the knowledge of what and who we are protecting (in Christ), we certainly should not allow ourselves to get hurt over and over again. We should no longer be like the millions of people who are constantly being hurt, often by the same sources.

Learn to take a different approach. If you have been hurt by someone before, then allowed them back into your life and find yourself getting happy over the same thing that hurt you before. *Stop* and *remember*. Do not let your emotions take you over and lead you right back to the same kind of pain. *Stop* and *remember* the trouble you experienced before.

Even though your feelings will challenge you and say "but things are different now," you must not allow yourself to be drawn back into those situations. Going back only demonstrates the fact that you have not changed. If you do decide to take the risk (like so many others do), first ask yourself, *Am I ready to go through all that pain again? Am I willing to experience the same thing all over again?*

Beloved, let us learn from our painful past. Our lessons should not be limited to learning to protect ourselves from being hurt all over again. We must also learn how to treat others, how to love and how to be gentle and honest to one another. If we don't learn to do these things, we may be the one who leaves someone in the same type of pain from which they (or we) were trying to escape.

Isaiah 40:31 tells us that we can defuse the pain of the past through Jesus. "But they that wait upon the Lord shall renew their strength; they shall mount up with wings as eagles; they shall run, and not be weary; and they shall walk, and not faint."

If left unresolved, your pain can lead to anger and then you can become a tool for the devil. To avoid unresolved anger, you must stop looking at yourself as a victim of all you are going through, and instead always keep in mind that the Bible says we are more than conquerors through Christ Jesus (Romans 8:37). If you confront your past, you will avoid inflicting your pain on someone else. Do not allow your pain to create a new victim out of someone else.

Being free from your pain may involve confronting others, such as family members or loved ones, releasing your pain and being healed.

James 5:6 encourages us to confess our faults one to another, and pray for one another, that we may be healed. Confessing about the way we hurt can break the power of the enemy. Releasing pain can break the yoke of depression, because unreleased pain is often the cause of depression. Many of our churches are full of people who are beaten down with depression, just because they do not know how to release their pain.

Those who do not know how to communicate outwardly often resort to inner monologues, and don't realize that suppressing everything is building up pressure. An explosion is sure to result if the pressure is not relieved in some way, often resulting in the person losing control and acting out in ways they will later bring regret.

During the first three years of my ministry, I missed many of my blessings. I wasn't the average preacher who grew up in the church and understood church protocol. So I decided that the right thing for me to do would be to go to an elder in the faith.

Now keep in mind that at that time I was not a mature preacher, not even in physical appearance. I was just looking for some answers.

In 1 Samuel 16:7, we are told that man looks on the

outward appearance and God looks on the heart. Now imagine wearing the clothing a "hoodlum" would wear, going to see a pastor and sharing that you are looking for some wisdom because you feel the call of God in your life to go into the ministry—especially if you had gone to the wrong leader like I did!

Imagine . . . being saved but not transformed in how you dress. Well, as you can imagine, I was highly judged, ignored and neglected—because of my appearance.

Then when I realized that my outward appearance was not gaining me any favor, I considered a different approach. I began using the telephone instead, but even that did not work because somewhere during the conversation I always brought up my past or where I came from. In fact, one leader I phoned told me that I should give up the few people I was pastoring and do something else.

Because of my encounters with the leaders to whom I was looking for counsel, I became afraid of all leaders. So, I began to seek the Lord; and I began to do things myself. I did not have any fellowship with any other churches; I separated myself from others (like many leaders do today). However, this isolation only brought more pressure, and I began to realize that no man is an island.

I thought that I was protecting myself from having to meet another leader like the ones who had not given me good counsel. That's what I thought! In actuality, because I assumed they were all the same, I missed out on many great leaders God had tried to send into my life to help me.

Having personally experienced rejection and received bad counsel, I now strive to always give the very best spiritual counseling to those who are in need. So the pain I suffered for a season yielded good fruit, instead of bad fruit. I learned to do good to someone else and not allow my painful experiences to create a new victim.

My answer to those who have been hurt by someone and may now be attempting to protect themselves by closing themselves off from other people is found in Luke 6:38: "Give, and it shall be given unto you; good measure, pressed down, and shaken together, and running over, shall man give into your bosom."

Your blessings come from God, but oftentimes they must first pass through a man before they can reach you. However, if you are not willing (and determined) to look beyond what you think you see in man, push beyond your pain and take chances, you will always miss your opportunities to be blessed. As long as we continue to make judgments of people that are based on the past actions of others, we will continue to miss out on the blessings. In order to receive the blessings, we must first be a blessing to others.

One of the greatest hurts comes when someone in whom we trust for help and guidance fails us. Now, we must not allow that to hinder us from progressing and pushing beyond our pain.

When I became steadfast in this, I not only began to see my blessings, but I also began to reap them!

However, unlike in my early years of ministry, I use more wisdom and knowledge when I open myself up to other people.

I do not forget that while man will fail us every time, God *never* fails. In reality, we have all failed each other in one way or another. In Psalm 55, it is evident that David was hurt by someone who was very close to him. In verses 6–7, David states, "And I said, Oh that I had wings like a dove! for then would I fly away, and be at rest. Lo, then would I wonder far off, and remain in the wilderness. Selah."

In verses 12–14, we are given more information about the person who hurt him, "For it was not an enemy that reproached me; then I could have borne it: neither was it he that hated me that did magnify himself against me; then I would have hid myself from him: But it was thou, a man mine equal, my guide, and mine acquaintance. We took sweet counsel together, and walked unto the house of God in company."

If we look we back to Psalm 55:4–5 we begin to see the gravity of how much pain David was feeling, "My heart is sore pained within me: and terrors of death are fallen upon me. Fearfulness and trembling are come upon me, and horror hath overwhelmed me." We can see here that David even came to the point where he wanted to die, feeling that death would release the pain; and this brought on fear and trembling.

In Psalm 55:7, David tells of how he thought about running away into the wilderness. However, I believe that David knew that to run away from his pain would be as fruitless as attempting to run away from his own shadow. Indeed, running will never work; we must face our pain head-on.

Like David, our pain may indeed cause us to want to run away. That is why we have so many people church hopping. They move to another church when they begin to feel like they are about to experience whatever has hurt them in the past. However, if these runners would face their pain and conquer it, they would not feel compelled to keep on trying to escape. We can see a comparison here in verses 12–14 where David shared how his close friend had hurt him, and to make matters even worse, they had gone to the same church together. But David chose to not run. However, many people have not followed David's example. Instead, they ran into the wilderness—that is, out of the church and back into the world. That, of course, was the devil's plan from the very beginning.

Keeping hurting people on the run is one of the tactics the enemy uses to hinder people from moving forward into their destiny.

I ask you this: *Why must you run?* You are not the guilty one. You just need to forgive those who have hurt you and continue to keep your eyes on where you are going.

The road on which we must travel is never a surprise to God. If we happen to find ourselves in a difficult part of our journey, we must do as David did. In Psalm 55:16, David cried out, "As for me, I will call upon God; and the Lord shall save me." So instead of complaining, David determined to ask for deliverance from his pain. As we read Psalm 55:17, we see that David was determined to be healed from his pain. Because his pain did not heal overnight, there was a struggle that required prayer at morning, noon and night. In Psalm 55:18, we see that deliverance took place. "He hath delivered my soul in peace from the battle that was against me: for there were many with me."

David won his battle by conquering his pain. Until you conquer your pain, you will not win the battle.

We will face some things in life that we must not take personally, if we want to go forward, that is.

Keep in mind that Romans 8:28 states that no matter how bad things might be, if you love God, He can turn all these things around for your good. It is also important to remember that God allows certain people to face painful situations so that they can later use their experiences to strengthen other people.

For example, let's take a closer look at Joseph, who was shown a vision of himself ruling over his father and brothers. At that time he did not realize the pain he would have to endure to help his own family. He was thrown into a pit, sold into slavery, denied his heritage and falsely accused by Potiphar's wife. And to top it off, he spent many years in prison.

God ordained him to go through all of that in order to save Joseph's family and a whole nation from starvation during the time of famine.

Paul said this in another way in 2 Corinthians 1:3–4, "Blessed be our God, even the Father of our Lord Jesus Christ, the Father of mercies, and the God of all comfort; Who comforteth us in all our tribulation, that we may be able to comfort them which are in any trouble, by the comfort wherewith we ourselves are comforted of God."

On the other hand, some kinds of pain are more difficult to talk about than others. Even so, we must even talk about those things that are hardest for us to discuss. This is crucial, because burying the pain can be harmful to your soul *and* your body. It's true! The destructiveness of bottled-up pain is not limited to our mind and emotions; it is also detrimental to our physical health. Unreleased pain leads to anger. Then, when we are angry, certain toxins are released into our blood stream and cause us to be afflicted by various ailments.

The pain can also lead us to be selfish. For example, people who decide to escape their pain through suicide, selfishly desert all those they have left behind.

Then there are other people who are called pain carriers; they carry other people's pain. In 2 Samuel 13, we see just how destructive carrying someone else's pain can be. As we read about David's children Amnon, Tamar and Absalom, we learn that Amnon played sick and raped his sister Tamar. Absalom then carried Tamar's pain for two years and because of that pain, he killed his brother Amnon.

One may wonder what drove Absalom to kill his brother two years later. Well, two years had passed, but the pain was still present, as if it had only happened yesterday. The longer Absalom kept the pain in, the more the pressure built up. If he had forgiven Amnon and allowed God to take care of the situation, he would not have killed his own brother.

Let us look at the pain of losing a child. In 2 Samuel

12, we read that the prophet Nathan went to the king David's palace to remind him of Uriah the Hittite. After stealing Uriah's wife, Bathsheba, David had murdered Uriah. Because of the evil that David had done, the Lord struck David's child with sickness. Even though David fasted and prayed for the child, the child died. After David learned that the child had died, David pushed beyond his pain and went on with his life. Verses 20–21 say, "Then David arose from the earth, and washed, and anointed himself, and changed his apparel, and came into the house of the Lord, and worshiped: then he came to his own house; and when he required, they set bread before him, and he did eat. Then said his servants unto him, What thing is this that thou hast done? thou didst fast and weep for the child, while it was alive; but when the child was dead, thou didst rise and eat bread."

In verses 22–23, David explains his response. "And he said, While the child was yet alive, I fasted and wept: for I said, Who can tell whether God will be gracious to me, that the child may live? But now, he is dead, wherefore should I fast? can I bring him back again? I shall go to him, but he shall not return to me."

To some people, what David did may look very cruel. However, because he realized that God was in control and not him, David let his son go. By doing so, he was released from his painful situation. Even his servants began to wonder why he stopped mourning.

David also encouraged himself by saying that even though his son could not return to him, he would go to his son (v. 23). David knew that his son was in the hands of the Lord.

Beloved, are you mourning for a loved one who has died in the Lord? Does the pain stop you from functioning in life? Are you unable to go to work because depression and frustration have overtaken you? Be comforted, dear friend, in the knowledge that God does not want your mourning to paralyze you. He wants you to live out your life here on earth. Encourage yourself like David did, keep in mind that when you have finished living down here, you will meet your loved one up there.

We must remember that pain will not come out unless we let it out; we cannot be healed if we continue to suppress our feelings. We need to communicate our true feelings. Some people who communicate inwardly expect others to somehow hear them outwardly. However, if we are willing to push outwardly—beyond our pain—God is willing to push away our circumstances and give us a miracle. We should not allow our pain to stop us from bringing forth the miracle that God has for us.

In some cases, people are unknowingly carrying pain they inherited from as far back as their great-grandparents. This process of inheriting pain lies in the truth that love begets love, hate begets hate, joy begets joy, happiness begets happiness, sorrow begets sorrow and pain begets pain.

Yes, pain can be passed down from one generation to another. Because of this, many people are experiencing pain but they do not realize where the pain is coming from. For example, people who have been hurt by their spouse or one of their parents may find themselves passing their pain on to their children in the form of anger, neglect or abuse.

When a person acts out of his hurt, he tends to do things that he later wishes he had never done. After he realizes that he acted out of his pain instead of out of a godly character, he regrets what he has done. However, in spite of his regret and apologies, he will continue to hurt others again and again, if he does not address the source of his problem. His conduct will remain the same until he has been healed from his pain.

Do you have a past or ongoing relationship that is causing you pain? If so, why do you allow this person to continue to inflict pain on you? Why would you self-destruct over a painful situation?

Uncontrolled anger is sometimes the root cause of some hidden or unresolved pain that we haven't faced. If you are suffering from this, you must allow the Holy Ghost to shine His light inside of you and expose every hidden intruder that seeks to keep you captive against your will. In 2 Timothy 2:26, we are told that we can recover ourselves out of the snares of the enemy if we have been taken captive by him. We must remember that the devil can only keep us where we want to stay. If you don't want to stay in pain, he must release you in the name of Jesus.

The Healer is right there with you. Just as the dog was there to lick Lazarus' wounds, the Holy Ghost is mending your wounds right now! He is doing a work in you right now. He wants you to be free. Be healed and be free! For whom the Son has set free, he is free indeed!

Building Up Yourself Through the Anointing

When I talk about building up yourself, I'm not referring to physical parts of the human body. When I say "self," I'm referring to the mind, spirit, body and soul (every emotion), all of which are the ingredients of a human life.

First things first; let us deal with the spirits that work destructively. Let us call them the trinity of destruction, the devil. Look at John 10:10. This scripture tells us that the thief (the devil) came not but to steal, kill and destroy. We can see through this passage of scripture that this spirit comes in with the intention of totally destroying us.

Before we were saved, this spirit had destroyed our emotions, bodies and minds. We must remember that even after people are saved, their emotions often remain unchanged.

Let us look at Isaiah 61:1 in a way we may have never seen it before: "The spirit of the Lord God is upon me; because the Lord hath anointed me to preach good tidings unto the meek; he hath sent me to bind up the brokenhearted, to proclaim liberty to the captives, and the opening of the prison to them that are bound." This and other portions of the Bible give us the proven fact that a man, woman or child's spirit, soul and body can be built up by the Spirit of God .

The Bible says that it wasn't Jesus who was doing the healing, even though we know that He is a Healer. It was the Holy Spirit, operating through Jesus, who was doing the healing. Beloved, this Spirit is still in action today.

He is ready to build us up in any area where we have been torn down by the enemy, if we would only open up those areas where we have been hurt, and allow Jesus to come in. In Romans 8:11, we read that the same Spirit that raised Jesus from the dead lives in those of us who are in Christ Jesus.

In order for us to be healed, we must first be willing to yield ourselves to the Spirit of God. We must know that He is the third part of the Trinity, which shows us that He is also a Person. He is the One who searches the heart and knows where every one of our difficulties lies. Because He also works through people, we must be willing to sense the Spirit while He is using someone else. One reason why this is important is because many people may be among you who are not well-known evangelists, but have the anointing upon their lives to heal.

The Bible states in Acts 10:38 that God anointed Jesus of Nazareth, who went around doing good and healing those who were oppressed by the devil. Many of our minds have been oppressed by the enemy, but the anointing of God can give us back our spiritual discernment.

We know from 2 Corinthians 4:4 that the mind of an unbeliever is blinded by the enemy. When a person comes to Christ, he must be transformed by the renewal of his mind. (See Romans 12:2.) Until the mind is renewed, the enemy will continue to manipulate that person, even if he is a believer. That is why Paul told us to pray for the feeble-minded who are amongst us.

Philippians 4:8 clearly describes what state our minds should be in, what things we should be thinking about. "Finally brethren, whatsoever things are true, whatsoever things are honest, whatsoever things are just, whatsoever things are pure, whatsoever things are lovely, whatsoever things are of good report; if there be any virtue, and if there be any praise, think on these things." Again, let us reflect on the fact that Paul encouraged us to govern our thoughts according to the word of God, because as a man "thinketh in his heart, so is he" (Prov. 23:7).

If we are not careful to build up our minds through God's Word, the enemy will take the opportunity to lead our minds to return back to operating in the old state. The mind is most important. The mind controls the body, and whatsoever the mind says, the spirit, body and soul—and every emotion—react to it. David encouraged us to meditate on the Word of God.

When we hear about meditation, we may tend to think of yoga or some other form of New Age religion. However, meditating on God's Word conforms our minds to His will and His ways.

For example, when the mind comes into maturity (growing up and being renewed in the mind of Christ), the person begins to give others the benefit of the doubt, not judging them without seeing their actions through the mind of Christ. Our minds should be trained to think the best of others, keeping in mind that God thinks the best of us. To understand the magnitude of this, we only have to look as far as considering how God demonstrated the high value He places upon us when He gave His Son as an offering for our sin.

That's why when we see the worst of a person, our minds should cause our mouths to speak the best of that person, in order to speak a word of change in his life. Ephesians 4:23 tells us to be renewed in the spirit of our minds.

Proverbs 18:14 says that the spirit of a man can sustain him in sickness. So if your spirit is strong, it can help you to overcome sickness in your body. The enemy tries to kill our spirit because if our spirit is weak, the body will become weak and then it will hard for us to function. For instance, before we can ever think of exercising, our spirit must be willing to exercise. If not, the body won't exercise. Remember, because the spirit is the driving force in the body, the body will only go as far as the spirit pushes it to go.

A lot of people make resolutions to exercise. Their bodies are willing to do so, but their spirits are too weak to continue. If change is to come in the body, it must first be built up in the spirit. Then the spirit will motivate the body to do what it doesn't want to do. Discipline starts in our spirit. Once discipline reigns in our spirit, the body then falls in line.

Paul encouraged us to not allow any guile (that is,

any yoke) to enter into our spirit. He further points out that guile hinders many from fulfilling their calling because of the weakness of the spirit. It is hard to confront the enemy when our spirit is weak.

Paul encouraged us to be strong so that we may be able to stand in the evil days. (See Ephesians 6:10–18.) When Paul said "be strong in the Lord" (v. 10), he was not just talking about the body, he was also referring to the spirit. Remember, fear comes through our spirit and then effects our body. Paul clearly stated in 2 Timothy 1:7 that God has not given us a spirit of fear, but of power, and of love and of a sound mind. We must remember the reason for the anointing is to build up those who are broken and to loose those who are in spiritual bondage. (See Isaiah 61:1–2.) The evil spirit that comes to steal, kill and destroy has deprived many from functioning the way they would want to. When the devil was at work in their lives, before they got saved, he had trodden over many minds, spirits, emotions and bodies, leaving many of them dysfunctional.

As a result, many Christians cannot function in whole and healthy ways because they have been robbed and victimized by the devil. In fact, the enemy has killed the joy of many a Christian.

Many are afraid to rejoice over something good because it brings back the memory of the world. Before, some of us used to rejoice when we thought we had something so good (whatever it might be), but then it would slip right out of our hands and bring us disappointment. You may wonder why so many Christians are still captive. In many cases, it is because their confidence has not been strengthened even though they are saved.

There are many Christians who believe that they do not deserve to ever have anything good. So many are saved, yet they are imprisoned by the spirit of the world. However, we must remember that we have the spirit of God in us to set us free. We must stand steadfast and confident in truth, no longer adhering to or responding to the lies of the enemy. The truth of the Word of God in Isaiah 10:27 states: "And it shall come to pass in that day, that his burden shall be taken from off thy shoulder, and his yoke from off thy neck, and the yoke shall be destroyed because of the anointing."

Yes, the anointing guarantees freedom and healing from the yoke (all of it) that the devil once placed on us. In this scripture, Isaiah is referring to an appointed time—and this is the appointed time: It is your time to be free! But despite the fact that our guarantee for healing was instituted through Jesus Christ over two thousand years ago, many people are missing the anointing that can build up their lives.

However, we have much to rejoice about. We can thank God that the season is still continuing right now. Remember, "Now unto him that is able to do exceeding abundantly above all that we can ask or think, according to the power that worketh in us" (Eph. 3:20). This scripture tells us that according to the power that is working in us, God is able to do more and greater things than we could even begin to imagine. Now that is something pure and lovely to think on!

This same anointing to both build up the church, and

to build up our lives so that we may operate as properly functioning parts of the body of Christ. Because the anointing is so crucial, we must stay in a church that has two very key components: The leaders must teach and preach on the power of the Holy Ghost, and the environment must be such that the praises of God must usher in the anointing.

We must make room for the presence of God. If we study Romans 8, we can see that wherever the Spirit of the Lord is, there is liberty. Stand firm in the fact that God wants you to be made whole; to be made whole in your mind, you body, your spirit and your soul (your emotions).

So why is it so important to stay in a church where the anointing is ushered in? Well, powerful things happen in the anointing. When the anointing shows up to destroy things like our depression, our fears and our low self-esteem, God's power can make us whole. His healing power is right there to build us up wherever we are broken. God will free us in those areas where we have been manipulated by the schemes and tricks of the devil. God wants us to be firm, and we can only be firm when we have built up those areas where we are insecure and crippled in our actions.

God's presence and anointing are not limited to the walls of any sanctuary. You can begin to confess God's anointing in those areas of your life right now.

Your healing can begin with you being honest about the areas where you are crippled or barren. That will devastate the power of the enemy's hold on those areas. Now confess who God says you are and not what you think you know or feel about yourself at this moment.

Change takes place during the time we are building up ourselves with the knowledge of God's Word and the anointing that is in our lives.

So I command those broken pieces in your life, in the name of Jesus, to come alive and be healed! You who are broken must know that you are loved, seen as precious and wonderfully created in the image of God.

See yourself as who God says you are and not what people say you are. Don't look upon the injuries that the devil has afflicted on you; just remember that those injuries will heal even though it will take time.

If I can be your personal counselor for a moment, I would like to encourage you to find a positive friend or loved one who will speak words of encouragement and healing into your life—someone who will be able to walk you through your healing, someone who will be patient with you while you are going through your personal pain.

Romans 8:26 shows us that the Spirit of God is willing and able to heal us from the infirmities or evil afflictions (infirmities) we have suffered. In Exodus 33:13, Moses prayed "Now therefore, I pray thee, if I have found grace in thy sight, shew me now thy way, that I may know thee, that I may find grace in thy sight: and consider that this nation is thy people."

The Lord responded in verse 14, "And he said, 'My presence shall go with thee, and I will give thee rest.'"

It is the spirit of God that will build us up and give us rest in every area of our lives. When we have our mind built up, our spirit is free from guile and our emotions are not being manipulated by the enemy; then our body, which houses these different elements, will be free to function and lead a clean, healthy life.

Building Back the Family Foundation

Too few of God's principles are being played out in today's families. This is why so many homes are broken by divorce and so many couples who do stay married live like roommates instead of living the family life.

To understand the importance of the family unit, we must consider God's original design of the family. And for the family unit to be the joyous institution that God meant for it to be, we must study and apply the biblical principles regarding the family.

A family is not merely a husband, wife and children, as many imagine it to be. It is more than just that. Number one, a family should be a school and a sanctuary. Schools and sanctuaries are places where we go to learn principles to be applied in our daily lives. That also means that we should not rely only on school teachers and government laws to teach us the morals that should actually be instilled in us through our families and in our homes.

Psalm 133:1 tells us to consider how good and pleasant it is for brethren to dwell in unity. We know that the devil divides, but God multiplies. In John 10:10 Jesus makes a statement where He contrasts the thief (the devil) and the good Shepherd (Jesus). "The thief cometh not, but for to steal, and to kill, and to destroy: I am come that they might have life, and that they might have it more abundantly." The word "life" in this text, does not only refer to life after death, it also refers to an abundant life here on earth, including being happy and living the original family life.

Some people are not happy having a family. They would prefer living a life with no responsibility. The staggering divorce rate of today reflects this line of thinking. If you feel that way, you are already trapped in the enemy's conspiracy to kill, steal and destroy.

Certainly, not all families are dysfunctional.

If we look very closely, we can find many happy, healthy families. But this seems to be the exception rather than the rule, even in the church. In fact, even our church leaders often fail to model family as God intended it to be. So where do we look for our example? We can only look to the righteous principles of God revealed in the Scriptures.

We read in Genesis chapter 1 about the first family, Adam and Eve, who were joined together by God in the garden of Eden. Their duty was to obey God's rule. By doing so, Adam and Eve lived hundreds of years blissfully—until they disobeyed God's rule. Genesis 3 shows us the fall of man after he did not follow the rule of God precisely. We should know that God's righteous principles are not in the Bible just to take up space; they are there to give us direction. Like Adam and Eve, a danger awaits us if we do not follow the principles of God.

For the family institution to be restored back to the

way it should be, *both* the husband and the wife must follow the principles of God. Husbands must first realize that they should love their wives even as Christ loved the church and gave Himself for it. (See Ephesians 5:25.) In so doing, husbands will enable and motivate their wives to submit to their husbands, as unto the Lord. (See Ephesians 5:22.)

When these principles are in place, the children will take on the same submissive spirit. But, if the husband is not loving his wife, then the wife will not want to submit, and the children will follow suit. When we do not follow these key principles, we open ourselves to a spirit of rebellion.

Wherever there is no order, there is disorder; and true order comes from the Word of God. In order for the wife to submit, she must love the Lord and refuse to see as the world sees. The world sees submission as slavery and abuse, but we are called to not be conformed to the world. In Romans 12:2, we are admonished, "And be not conformed to this world: but be ye transformed by the renewing of your mind, that ye may prove what is good, and acceptable and perfect, will of God."

For a woman to be encouraged by Titus 2:5, "To be discreet, chaste, keepers at home, good, obedient to their own husbands, that the word of God be not blasphemed," she must look at the Scriptures from God's point of view and not the world's.

In so doing, she will not take on a spirit of witchcraft, which is a result of a rebellious nature. When we rebel against the will of God, a spirit of witchcraft is automatically dispatched against us.

There are many couples who are under the control of witchcraft because they have the attitude that if one partner is not obeying God, the other should do the same, forgetting that it was God who laid down the rule. So, there are many men who stopped loving their wives because they do not submit, and there are many women who refuse to reverence their husbands because the husbands are not loving them as they ought to.

It is our duty, whether man or woman, to own up to our responsibility to the Word of God, knowing that Ephesians 5:21 states that we are to submit one to the other in the fear of God. If the couple truly loves the Lord, they will learn to see it God's way. However, that is one of the problems in many marriages—we refuse to see it God's way.

One common reason why a husband cannot love the way he ought to and a wife cannot submit the way she ought to is because they have fallen out of love with God. Before getting married, they were in love with God. But then somehow, some way, they fell out of love with God and now the husband and wife only have superficial love for each other.

Because they have fallen out of love with God, they cannot follow God's Word like they used to. This, in turn, affects every area of their lives, including their marriage and family life. We should not forget to keep fueling our love for God even when we are married. Being in love with God will keep us faithful to His will and His desires, even during times of difficulty. For example, a man who is in love with God will then love his "un-submissive" wife. Likewise, a wife who is in love with God will love the husband who does not love her the way he should.

We should know that it was the power of God's love that brought change into our lives. So if we desire a healthy and happy family, God must remain the first priority in our lives. When God is our first priority, His overflowing love is flowing through us, teaching us how to love our spouse and our children and spend quality time with them. Investing love, time, energy and prayer in our children helps us to shape their lives according to Proverbs 22:6, "Train up a child in the way he should go: and when he is old, he will not depart from it."

Whatever spirit rules the head in the home will eventually rule the whole house. Paul encouraged us in 1 Timothy 2:1 to pray for our leaders. "I exhort therefore, that, first of all, supplications, prayers, intercessions, and giving of thanks, be made for all men; For kings, and for all that are in authority; that we may lead a quiet and peaceable life in all godliness and honesty."

Paul is saying that prayer should be made for all those in leadership. We can expand that to include leaders in the household. Prayer is the key to a quiet and peaceable life. Therefore, the wife should not attempt to control the head of the house, but should instead pray for God to lead the husband the proper way. There are many wives who think that their prayers do not count because of the attitude of their husband.

But James 5:16b explains that the "effectual fervent prayer of a righteous man [or woman] availeth much."

The wife must stay in prayer, asking God that her husband be led by the Spirit of God and not by the enemy. The greatest problem in families is that the majority of the husbands do not take the time to learn how to deal with their wives according to knowledge. And because so many do not take the time to learn about their wives, they become frustrated and bitter against them. The mistake that many husbands often make is that they try to change their wives instead of learning how to accept them on their level of spiritual maturity.

Jesus told the disciples to pray that they enter not into temptation. Prayer is the key to stop divorce. Divorce does not just hurt the husband and wife; but it also hurts the children. Too many families spend too little (if any) time in prayer. While the husband is too busy working or involved in "extracurricular" activities and the wife is too busy working and taking care of the home, the children are left to fend for themselves. And soon, husband, wife and children grow apart from each other.

Many people don't know what it is to have a family life. They may have been raised by babysitters or shuffled between relatives and friends—and some were even raised by the television set. Before having a family, we must make a commitment that our children will not be raised by someone (or something) else because we are either too lazy or think we're too busy to parent our children ourselves. We, the parents, have much to teach our children that should not be taught by babysitters, teachers or the media. Teaching our children should include respecting their teachers and police officers, and saying "thank-you" and "excuse me." The dinner table should remain an important part of family life. Regularly having dinner at the dinner table with our children (without interruptions) is a wonderful place to enjoy each other, to teach, to learn, to share, to love and to be thankful.

In some families, the husband does not know how to love his wife or children because he did not have certain family values instilled in him. In some cases, he may have grown up without a family. In such a situation, the wife may have to be the one to teach and instill godly values within the family.

Becoming the family that God wants us to be will requires a lot of patience. Wives should be patient with their husbands, husbands should be patient with their wives and both parents should be patient toward their children.

Because the family is intended to be a solid foundation for our lives, we must work toward making the family life the best that it can be. We must stand against immorality that is exploiting our youth through the world system. And in all things that we do, let us not forget to pray together. In Luke 18:1, we learn that Jesus taught that men should always pray and not faint. Prayer is a necessary and important part of a secure family life. I believe the old saying . . . *those who pray together, stay together!*

Yes, prayer and obedience to the principles of God

are keys to having the abundant life that Jesus came to earth to offer us. That life that is only possible through Him and by staying in love with Him, being honest with ourselves, staying open and obedient to God, standing firm in the anointed life God has destined us to, and being a blessing to others. Then, and only then, we can be and remain whole—in spirit, soul and body.

My dear friend, "Wilt thou be made whole?"

Part II

Your Wilderness Experience: Finding the Good In It

Snakes, sand, scorching sun and endless miles of dry treacherous terrain—these are things that often come to mind when we think of the wilderness. We may see the wilderness as a desert, a dangerous place of discomfort and lack, a place where we have to struggle to survive. Most Christians can probably relate to having a wilderness experience—a dry season, at some point in their walk with the Lord. During a wilderness experience, we face tests, trials, temptations and tribulations; and we are usually in great need of direction and strength.

Though we encounter these unpleasant conditions, as children of God, we should not perceive our journey through the wilderness as merely a phase where we just barely exist and survive. The wilderness can be a place of establishment and maturation. It is a place where you can learn to trust and depend on God. In the midst of your wilderness you can allow the Lord to prepare you for a place of abundance. Although traveling on a wilderness journey may not be altogether a happy time, you can find good in it.

To begin, let us consider Moses' life. Remember that Moses was brought up in the house of Pharaoh (Heb. 11:24). In Moses' natural life he was blessed.

However, spiritually, he was poor. After he left the riches and wealth of Pharaoh, Moses began to face the reality of life. After tasting the rough experiences, Moses decided that he would rather "suffer affliction with the people of God, than to enjoy the pleasures of sin for a season" (Heb. 11:25).

This goes to show that no matter who you are, you have to experience the wilderness for yourself. God does not want you to depend upon the things you possess, but on Him. The Bible clearly tells us to "...seek ye first the kingdom of God, and his righteous; and all these things shall be added unto you" (Matt. 6:33).

Moses received his calling in the wilderness. He left everything he had in Egypt. Yet while he was in the wilderness, thinking that he was just doing a natural work (working for his father-in-law Jethro), Moses was being trained for a spiritual purpose. (See Exodus 3:2–10.) His calling would be from the natural sheep to spiritual sheep. Moses was trained in the wilderness for forty years before receiving his calling. Just imagine the great sacrifices Moses had to make. He had lived for forty years with the riches and wealth in the land of Egypt. But he had to give up this luxurious lifestyle and spend forty more years in the wilderness without such riches.

The wilderness is simply a place where you must trust in God. God takes you through the wilderness in order to build you, to train you and to equip you for His work.

"But the God of all grace, who hath called us unto his eternal glory by Christ Jesus, after that ye have suffered a while, make you perfect, establish, strengthen, settle you" (1 Pet. 5:10).

We should be mindful of these verses in Deuteronomy 8:2–5:

> And thou shalt remember all the way which the LORD thy God led thee these forty years in the wilderness, to humble thee, and to prove thee, to know what was in thine heart, whether thou wouldest keep his commandments, or no. And he humbled thee, and suffered thee to hunger, and fed thee with manna, which thou knewest not, neither did thy fathers know; that he might make thee know that man doth not live by bread only, but by every word that proceedeth out of the mouth of the LORD doth man live. Thy raiment waxed not old upon thee, neither did thy foot swell, these forty years. Thou shalt also consider in thine heart, that, as a man chasteneth his son, so the LORD thy God chasteneth thee.

Now we see that the children of Israel were chosen as an example for all nations. But after they were chosen, they had to be readied, equipped and tested, so that God's glory could be seen in them. First Peter 4:12–13 reads:

> Beloved, think it not strange concerning the fiery trial which is to try you, as though

some strange thing happened unto you: But rejoice, inasmuch as ye are partakers of Christ's sufferings; that, when his glory shall be revealed, ye may be glad also with exceeding joy.

But the children of Israel rebelled against God's plan because their hearts were not with God. They mourned and complained in the wilderness and many of them died.

God hates for anyone to murmur, because murmuring stops the Lord from working on the things in our lives that need to be changed. In fact, the scripture tells us that ". . . all things work together for good to them that love God, to them who are the called according to his purpose" (Rom. 8:28).

My fellow brethren of the LORD, as chosen and called for a time like now to go forth in His power and glory, while you are in the wilderness of your Christian life, know this:

To everything there is a season, and a time to every purpose under the heaven: A time to be born a time to die; A time to plant, and a time to pluck up that which is planted; A time to kill, and a time to heal; a time to break down, and a time to build up; A time to weep, and a time to laugh; a time to mourn, and time to dance; A time to cast away stones, and a time to gather stones together, a time to embrace, and a time to refrain from embracing; A time to get, and a time to lose; a time to keep, and a time to cast away; A time to rend, and a time to sew; a time to keep silence, and a time to speak; A time to love, and a time to hate; a time of war and a time of peace.

—ECCLESIASTES 3:1–8

As we all know, before we get to the Promised Land, we must first go through the wilderness. We can recall Jesus' experience in the wilderness. Jesus, who was God in the flesh, had to go through the wilderness Himself. As God, He "made himself of no reputation, and took upon him the form of a servant, and was made in the likeness of men: And being found in fashion as ;a man, he humbled himself, and became obedient   " (Phil 2:7–8).

As we see in Luke 4:2, when Jesus was at a weak point, he still obeyed God. Here, Jesus used the Word while He was in the wilderness. As Christians, we must know what the Word of God says about strength. When we are going through the wilderness we must keep the joy of the Lord, for the joy of the Lord is our strength. Many times we will be tempted, as Jesus was. But as we are trampled, we must concentrate on God's Word and His will for our lives.

Know that the devil comes with empty promises and tries to distract us from having an effective walk with the Lord. We must remember that while Jesus was in the wilderness, he was not complaining. Instead, He was powerfully speaking the Word of God.

We must *always* use the Word to rebuke the devil when he comes to draw us away from God's will. In Luke 4:14, Jesus returned from the wilderness in the power of the Spirit and began the work that the Father had sent Him to do.

Before anyone can truly experience the glory of the Lord, he must go through a suffering experience. Our God, who is the God of the mountains, is the same God in the valley. We should not be like the children of Israel who failed their test in the wilderness.

We must know that in the wilderness there are no fine restaurants, expensive cars or gold jewelry. In the wilderness, we will get only what God sees as our needs. But, if we enjoy such an experience, it will be easy for us to see the hands of God.

If we remain faithful with the blessings of God, He will make us rulers over many. When we learn to be grateful for the old car we have, God will give us a new one.

If we are appreciative of a few church members, God will give us many members. Whatever may seem small right now, if we just remain faithful until God opens the windows of heaven, He will give us a blessing that we would not have room enough to receive.

As we examine Jesus' life in the wilderness, we see three major principles that will also hold true for us:

1. Jesus was totally obedient to God, even at His weakest point.
2. Jesus fully trusted God's Word.

3. Jesus received the reward of coming out
   with the power of the Spirit.

The children of Israel went through a wilderness
where some of them were bitten by snakes, swallowed
up by earthquake and even died. I believe that this was
the same type of wilderness that Jesus went through.
Jesus went through a wilderness with many snakes, no
water and no food, yet He was able to stay there for
forty days and forty nights. Comparatively speaking,
the children of Israel could have come out of the
wilderness within eleven days, but because they
refused to obey God, their stay in the wilderness was
prolonged. Actually, many of the Israelites never made
it out of the wilderness, while it took the others forty
years. Just think, forty years, as opposed to Jesus' experience of forty days and nights. I believe Jesus' humility
and His yielding to allow God to have His way,
enabled Him to come out triumphantly.

Whenever we are in the wilderness, God wishes to
shape and mold us. We should seek Him for His purpose of our lives. When we humble ourselves, God will
bring us out victoriously.

As I shared in the introduction of this book, before
the Lord saved me, I sold drugs on the streets of Boston,
making lots of money, buying fine cars and expensive
jewelry. I always had money. But, when I surrendered
my life to Jesus, He stripped me of all my worldly pos-
sessions.

My financial loss came little by little. It happened in
small increments. Remember, God doesn't put too

much pressure on us. He only takes us through what we can bear. Whatever God does is perfect. Our God is sovereign and a God of perfect timing. As I awoke spiritually, I realized I had been stripped completely. All my clothes, cars, gold, money and sweethearts were gone. At first, I was in a state of confusion.

I could not understand how all my belongings had disappeared so quickly. At that point in my life, I was not knowledgeable about God's Word. It was my faith and determination that kept me strong until I began to search the Word. Then, my strength increased as I read about David.

I read 1 Samuel 26:1–3, and understood that after David was chosen by God to be king of Israel, Saul was being used by the devil to chase David in the wilderness. Nevertheless, David never gave up on God while in the wilderness. From David's own experience in the wilderness, he was able to write several portions of the Book of Psalms.

Even while being confused, David still unwaveringly trusted in the God of Abraham, Isaac and Jacob. David's leadership gifts, as well as the plan of God, were being manifested while he was in the wilderness.

So, while I was awakening spiritually, I became encouraged as I saw how David trusted God, came out from the wilderness and become the king of Israel. As a result, I was encouraged to hold on. In my years of being saved, I realized that sometimes, only in the wilderness can one hear the voice of God clearly.

As the apostle Paul received his calling on the road to Damascus, he did not go to any man. Instead, he went out in the wilderness of Arabia to hear even more from God. Paul came out of the wilderness not only knowing about law, but also about grace.

I believe that just as Jesus was led by the Spirit in the wilderness (see Matthew 4:1), to be prepared for the Father's work, Paul was also led into the wilderness of Arabia to be prepared for the work of Jesus Christ.

As we study the life and ministry of John the Baptist, we see that he spent much of his life in the wilderness, preparing and carrying out his mission as a forerunner for the Messiah, Jesus.

In the wilderness of our Christian life is where we see the glory of God and where we experience the manifestation of the presence of God. If we look closely at what we are facing—the trials, the ups and downs and our tribulations—we realize that only God can enable us to overcome the things we face.

We must remember that we are called as soldiers for Christ (see 2 Timothy 2:1–3), to overcome the trials that we face, knowing that Jesus said He will never leave or forsake us. Sometimes God allows us to live with less than what we thought we could live with, so that we may always give Him the glory and the praise. We must know that our God does not spoil us, as our mothers and fathers may sometimes spoil us. He gives us manna, and if we appreciate the manna, He increases our blessing.

If we look closely at the life of Jesus according to the gospels, we see that after ministering and healing the sick, He would go back to the wilderness or a place where he could pray. So that he would not lose touch with the Father, He would separate Himself from the others and spend time alone with Him. During this time of prayer He would hear from the Father, and then afterward, He would minister effectively to those who were sick.

When God is leading us into a time in the wilderness to strip away the things that are hindering us from serving Him effectively, the mistake we often make is to lean on our own understanding. But, Proverbs 3:5–6 states, "Trust in the Lord with all thine heart; and lean not unto thine own understanding. In all thy ways acknowledge him, and he shall direct thy path."

The scripture says that we should not think according to the way we once thought or felt. If we continue to go by our feelings, we will never understand what God is planning for our lives. And 1 Corinthians 5:7 states that we "...walk by faith, not by sight." That means we shall walk strictly in the light of God's Word.

From the beginning of time, the devil has been using the same tricks, but with numerable variations. Genesis 2:16–17 states that Adam and Eve should not eat from the tree of the knowledge of good and evil. We know that God's command was for their own good, but they were deceived by the devil and disobeyed God.

Today Satan plays his same old strategy on the people of God, attempting to get us into a place where we would disobey God and obey him instead. He always attempts to interfere with what God is doing in our lives. When God is doing a work in us by keeping us for a season in the wilderness, the devil often shows up carrying a desire that is not from the heart of God. While what he brings may appear appealing, it is actually an evil scheme to pull us away from the will of God.

Many of God's people are being deceived by the natural things of the world. We must remember that God has given us power over these tactics that the devil was even using against us before we got saved. We would sometimes wonder, why we the Christians, have to go through pain and tribulation now that we are saved. Sometimes we are surprised by our circumstances because we did not expect to still be faced, at times, by the same things we faced before we were saved.

Now allow me to explain this to you: There is a big difference between suffering for the devil and suffering for God. The devil brings suffering as a device and scheme to kill, steal and destroy. When you suffer for the devil it brings pain, destruction and condemnation, and there is nothing to be accomplished. However, suffering for God brings blessing, light and life. Suffering for Him accomplishes the work of God in your life, and brings testimony of and appreciation for God's grace.

When the blessing does come, we must be careful to not worship the blessing or allow it to control us. On the contrary, our response must be to praise and adore the One from whom all blessings flow.

When we are living in Him, even those things that the devil meant for evil will be turned around in such a way that it brings good and brings glory to God. For example, you may have at one time suffered something very tragic before you were saved or even after salvation, such as molestation or rape. Maybe it is affecting you now and you are having a hard time forgiving the perpetrator. All that you have suffered and are suffering can be turned around by God for good. God can turn your pain into joy and your tragedy into triumph.

God can heal your wound that constantly hurts, if only you would just put your trust in Him. You might have even been raped by a total stranger or someone you trusted. You may have been abandoned by family or friends; perhaps you have been sick for a long period of time. Whatever your hardship, whatever your pain, you can safely put your trust in the fact that with Jesus, all things are possible.

In Luke 8:27–39, the Bible tells us about a man that was possessed by a demon named "Legion." The word *legion* means "a military force containing three to six thousand soldiers." In this case it means three to six thousand evil spirits. This tormented man lived in the wilderness and his life was troubled in every area.

We later see that after everything he had been through, he received healing from Jesus, who then used him in the ministry. This man was the first missionary in that region to be sent out to tell the people what God had done for him (vv. 38–39).

Let us look closely at this man. He, figuratively, came from rags to riches, from a life of torment and pain to a life of joy and peace. He was rewarded for all the things he had been through. We know that God would do the same things for us.

As we read the Scriptures, we see how Jesus healed

the sick and at times told them not to say anything (e.g., Matt. 8:1–4). However, in this case, he specifically told this man at the country of the Gadarenes to go and tell the people what God had done for him.

I believe that in this man's situation, he was being prepared for the work of God, but during his time of suffering and torment, he did not know it. I also believe that God sometimes does the same thing with us. As we face certain obstacles in life, we know that our God is love and does not need to explain anything to us.

He only wants us to obey Him—as Commander in Chief of our lives. The Bible tells us that trials come to make us stronger. We do not like trials, but they come to accomplish something in our lives. In Luke 1:37, the angel told Mary "For with God nothing shall be impossible." We have the assurance that God will bring us through the pressure we face.

God uses the things we dislike to shape us. It is *always* best to submit to the will of God and not wrestle or complain about the situation. The Lord told the prophet Jeremiah, "Before I formed thee in the belly I knew thee; and before thou camest forth out of the womb I sanctified thee, and I ordained thee a prophet unto the nations" (Jer. 1:5).

God never makes mistakes! God always knows where we are at in our wilderness. He ordained some things to happen to us. He is fully aware of what we are going through. The Bible says that He was touched by our infirmities and pain. I believe the reason we must go through our wilderness is for God to make us all what He wants us to be. We are called to be His ambassadors. Consider this: the children of Israel could not be exactly what God wanted them to be because they were always complaining about their circumstances.

Now let us look at Matthew 6:32–33. We see that our Father knows our needs because the Bible says "your heavenly Father knoweth that ye have need of all these things. But seek ye first the kingdom of God, and his righteousness; and all these things shall be added unto you." God's love is still the same, even when we're facing difficulties we don't understand.

We sometimes think that we are all alone living this Christian life. We must remember that our God is an omnipresent God. He is here, there and everywhere. He is intangible; He cannot be touched, but His Spirit shows up to bring comfort and peace.

In 2 Corinthians 12:9, the Lord Jesus told Paul that ". . . My grace is sufficient for thee: for my strength is made perfect in weakness."

The Lord is saying to us that His grace is enough and His strength is able to keep us even when we are at our weakest point. We often see that only in our weakest times does God display His power at just the right moment so that our faith can arise.

I myself have experienced a time of waiting on the Lord in which I could not go by feelings; I could only go by faith. While we wait on the Lord, we must encourage ourselves with His Word so that our feelings do not interfere with what God is doing in our lives. We must continue to have faith in His divine work.

Isaiah 43:2 states, "When thou passest through the waters, I will be with thee; and through the rivers, they shall not overflow thee: when thou walkest through the fire, thou shall not be burned; neither shall the flame kindle upon thee." God takes us through the wilderness to conform us to His ways and to strip us of our selfishness.

In Isaiah 40:31, we read about waiting on the Lord. We should keep occupied until He shows up, just as the disciples did. When the Lord told them to go and tarry in Jerusalem until the promise came, He meant for them to continue seeking God until the blessing came (Luke 24:49).

Psalm 66:10–12 states, "For thou, O God, hast proved us: thou has tried us, as silver is tried. Thou broughtst us into the net; thou laidst affliction upon our loins. Thou has caused man to ride over our heads; we went through fire and through water: but thou broughtest us out into a wealthy place."

We can begin to see clearly only when we are trusting and obeying God. When we do not understand things yet trust and obey Him, God leads us into a better environment: a place of holiness and purity so that we can live the fullness of life that He has given to us.

We must always know that the Father wants what is best for us. In order for God to give us the best, He has to take us through the places where we don't want to go: places where we don't always understand everything.

The children of Israel were at their happiest points

n they were getting their needs met. But when they
re in want, they could not see what God was doing
in their lives, so they rebelled. But God does not want
us to be like that. He wants us to be firm no matter
what situation we are facing. As Paul states in
Philippians 4:11, "Not that I speak in respect of want,
for I have learned, in whatsoever state I am, therewith
to be content."

Even though the children of Israel could not see
what was going on, we can learn by looking back at
what they did and did not do. We often think that we
learn by looking forward, but we only learn as we look
back at history. By taking heed to what history and
examples tell us, we will not make the mistakes the
children of Israel made, mistakes which caused them
to be destroyed in the wilderness.

The Bible has many examples of people who went
through a wilderness experience. Sarah was also in a
wilderness experience. The Bible states that Sarah was
barren and could not have a baby. In those days,
women who could not conceive a child were mocked
and ridiculed, because it was a disgrace for a woman to
be infertile.

Genesis 21:1 states that "the LORD visited Sarah just
as he had said, and the LORD did unto Sarah as he had
spoken."

Hanna was also barren, and she was also ridiculed
for not having a baby. But God answered Hanna at the
right time! (See 1 Samuel 5:17.)

We must realize that in our wilderness, we, too,
must wait *expectantly* for God to fulfill His promises

and bring forth miracles.

Remember His encouraging words in Isaiah 43:19: "Behold, I will do a new thing, now it shall spring forth; shall ye not know it? I will even make a way in the wilderness, and rivers in the desert."

Believe His promises and expect to see them fulfilled as you wait. Realize that in waiting, you can receive revelation from the Father. We get to know Him more when we wait properly. Waiting enables us to truly hear His voice when He speaks and to feel His love as he comforts and encourages us.

I sincerely believe that it is God's will for all of us, as God's people, to face tests and trials for a reason.

There are some saints who are more likely to stray away when they become too comfortable. You may find yourself so comfortable in God's work that you don't pray anymore, not realizing that you are really slip-sliding away from God. God will sometimes allow things to happen in order to get your attention.

There are some who are simply too busy to seek God because of their tight schedule with their children, job, the phone, house, taking care of themselves, appointments that have to be met and so on. All of this running around only hinders us from doing the will of God. Sometimes, the Lord slows us down to bring us to the place where He can lead us.

First Peter 5:6–7 gives us an example of how God wants to lead us. If we remain humble, the Father can effectively work through our lives. In addition, God wants to exalt His people after He accomplishes His work in us.

As we look at the forty days and nights of Jesus in the wilderness in Matthew 4, we notice that Jesus went into the wilderness to be tested before fully walking in His ministry. As He came out of His test, His fame increased, and He began to minister.

We should look at our trials as a boot camp, requiring us to go through different steps before we graduate. Each of these steps will lead us closer to our blessing as we mature in Christ. While we are being tested, we should not allow the spirit of fear to grip us, because fear will cause us not to finish our journey. It will cause us to doubt God.

The devil has stolen from us and deprived us, but our pain and suffering prepare us to regain all that God has for us. We must take note that our trials lead us closer to Jesus. The closer we get to Him, the more we will be purified and sanctified for a greater work.

Galatians 6:9 states that we should "not be weary in well doing: for in due season we shall reap, if we faint not." We must understand that our suffering enables us to experience things we never have experienced before. In order to sow back into other's lives what we have learned while in our wilderness, we must take into account all of the things that God has brought us through. Recalling the victories God has given unto us also helps us to remain focused as we press through our trying times.

The children of Israel's problem was that while they were in their wilderness, they could not see an end to their journey, so they would cry and complain. This would only hinder the move of God in their lives. They did not remember all the miracles God had done for them previously. So, if you don't want to go anywhere in life, if you want to be stagnant, unsuccessful, unproductive, and unfruitful, just keep complaining as they did.

Beloved, we must remember that our God is a moving God, and during the times that we cannot see our way out, we should never hinder the movement of God in our lives, as the children of Israel did. We must always continue to move with God.

In Exodus 14, we see that Moses and the Israelites could not escape Egypt because of the Red Sea, yet God opened the Red Sea for them! Here we see that when you trust God, He will meet your needs. God will not allow you to suffer more than you can handle.

Hebrews 13:8 states that "Jesus Christ is the same yesterday, and today, and forever." And Malachi 3:6 states, "For I am the LORD, I change not." Whatever God has to do for His elect, He will do. Like Moses and the children of Israel, just stand and see the salvation of God. Let us trust Him; He will never fail us.

I know that there are times in our trials when we look for God to show up and do the miraculous. When He does not perform the way we want Him to, we get confused. We also look for people to understand the test we are going through, and we cannot always understand or explain the things that God is doing in our lives. Fortunately, we find an example of such a situation in Job.

As we look at Job, we see there were unexplainable things happening to him. (See Job 1.) Note in Job

2:11–13 that Job kept quiet and did not try to explain what was going on with him. Ultimately, Job allowed God to have His way in his life. In the final analysis, God blessed Job twice as much as before. (See Job 42:10.)

God never leads us into the wilderness to cause us to fail; He leads us there to teach us to overcome. In the Book of Genesis, chapter 22, Abraham was tested. But after his test, it was proven that he loved God, and a blessing was released, according to verses 16–18. Our suffering is not only for patience, but also to show God how much we love Him.

We see that Jesus came out of the wilderness with power after His first test. (See Luke 4:14.) Suffering produces power in our lives, as well as spiritual blessings and natural blessings. It's the Father's will to bless us, but there are spiritual principles we have to follow in order for God's blessings to be released.

In Deuteronomy 7:12–13, we read of the blessing God gives us when we walk in His principles:

> Wherefore it shall come to pass, if ye hearken to these judgments, and keep, and do them, that the LORD thy God shall keep unto thee the covenant and the mercy which he sware unto thy fathers: And he will love thee, and bless thee, and multiply thee: he will also bless the fruit of thy womb, and the fruit of they land . . .

We must understand that when we are being tried,

God evaluates us to see if we are going to give in to the enemy or serve Him. If we choose to give in to the enemy, God will honor the choice that we make. But if we choose to serve the Lord, He will bless us accordingly. Deuteronomy 30:19 states, "I have set before you life and death, blessing and cursing: therefore choose life, that both thou and thy seed might live."

While we are walking in the wilderness of our own life experiences, we must look for things to encourage us as we endeavor to finish the race. When we feel frustrated, we must call upon God for strength and patience. We must remain faithful while we are walking in our wilderness. And we must always look for the positive and not allow what we see to distract us.

While some of us are in our furnace of affliction, we should look closely at our Christian life, for our trial is building Godly character. It make us more patient and give us more compassion. We are grieved, heavy burdened and tempted as the forces of darkness come against us. This is not the time to run in to our foxhole or to complain and cry, but this is the time to call on the name of Jesus, pray and talk to someone about the way we feel and what we are experiencing. We cannot predict how long our trials will last, but we can expect the fourth man to show up in our furnace of affliction, as he did for Shadrach, Meshach and Abednego. (See Daniel 3:25.) And that fourth man is Jesus. (This is an example of a Christophony, an appearing of the Christ in the Old Testament.)

Let us look at the prophet Habakkuk. Habakkuk had a burden or a vision from God, and at some point, because of pressure and what he saw, he truly forgot what God had shown him. (See Habakkuk 1:1–5.) But we ourselves have been down this road many times, when God has shown us things to come, but what we are facing causes us to forget. Yet we must know that God's word must come to pass because God's words (promises) are yea and amen.

In Habakkuk's frustration, we see where he denounced the law of God, saying that it does not work. In our time of pain and frustration, we sometimes think the same thing. But we must have faith. In fact, whatever trial Habakkuk was facing, it was worked out for his own good. Therefore, we must never get weary while we wait on God.

While we are walking in our wilderness, we must remain faithful so God can work on the weaknesses in our lives. In Exodus 14:10, we see that God was testing the children of Israel when Pharaoh's chariots cornered them between Pharaoh and the Red Sea. Fearful for their lives, they saw the incident as danger, but God had a plan to get glory out of their testing.

Although the devil will try to confuse and intimidate us, we should always know that our test is for the glory of God. And we must know that when we are being tested, it is the plan of the enemy to stop what God is doing in our lives. Remember what the Lord told Moses: "be still and know that I am God." I believe God meant, "you should know me by the miracles that I've done in Egypt; wait on me." God wants us to come out of our trials experiencing His goodness and, most of all, knowing Him more.

To the children of Israel in the wilderness during the time of testing, it seemed the test would last forever. But in Exodus 15:1, there was a rejoicing season. We must be reminded that after every testing, there is a promotion.

As our suffering increases, more anointing comes into our lives. The more we suffer for the will of Christ, the stronger we become spiritually. This is how we can know Him and have the assurance that He will neither leave us nor forsake us. (See Hebrews 13:5.)

While on their way to the Promised Land, the children of Israel only looked at two things— 1) their old way of life back in Egypt, and 2) their uncomfortable circumstances in the wilderness. Looking to Egypt was a desire to go back into the bondage from which the Lord had delivered them, and looking at their circumstances caused them to doubt God. We must not keep our eyes on what we see because what we see is temporal.

When we are facing things that we don't understand, we should make sure our thoughts agree with the Word of God. (See Philippians 4:8.) We cannot allow our thoughts to interrupt the plan that God has for our lives. Proverbs 23:7 says, "For as he thinketh . . . so is he." Our thoughts can control our feelings, whatever they are. In order to follow the Lord in our trials, we must be encouraged by the Word of God and meditate upon the promises of God.

At times it may seem impossible to meditate upon the Word of God because the devil opposes you. But don't give up.

Our God doesn't cause evil things to happen, but He uses evil things to shape us. In the wilderness, the children of Israel saw their test as evil because they could not understand why God took them through a place where they had hunger and thirst. But in fact, it was for their making. We must realize that whatever we face in life, God will use it for good.

We often try to understand everything that God is doing in our life, but Isaiah 55:8–9 lets us know that our thoughts are not his thoughts nor our ways His ways. For this reason, we must be confident that God is in complete control of everything we face, so we must remain confident as we face our sufferings. God is a God of wisdom and power. Therefore, let us keep a positive attitude when we face things that we cannot understand.

I believe God's children often give up too quickly, sometimes even before facing a real challenge. We must know that in order to have a testimony, we must depart our wilderness experience with wisdom. It is very important for us to earnestly face certain things in our lives for our benefit and the benefit of others. I believe it would be difficult to effectively encourage others without gathering wisdom from our own personal experiences.

We must be a living sacrifice, and a living sacrifice does not want to lie down on a burning altar. It normally tends to resist. We ourselves do not want to stay in our wilderness too long, but God will keep us in the wilderness until we lose pride and stubbornness and learn to appreciate His blessings.

We must keep our joy while we are facing hardship. Let us look at Sarah as she waited on the Lord and was visited at the appointed time as He had spoken in Genesis 21:1. God has an appointed time to bring us out of our wilderness, but until then, we must wrestle until our change comes. We must continue to have faith and patience.

In the Greek text, the word *patience* is a fruit that grows only under trials. So the wilderness is for the growth of our patience. It keeps us waiting on the promises of God, as we do know that our suffering can cause us to grieve. However, our grief increases along with wisdom according to Ecclesiastes 1:18.

There are many who think they are suffering above their level and for those who think they suffer too much, they need to examine their lives

If we're suffering as a result of our own sins, the suffering brings misery. However, if we suffer for Christ's sake in the will of God, the suffering takes us from glory to glory and increases God-like character in our lives. We must believe that the closer we remain to God's will in our wilderness, the closer we are to coming out. God will not allow us to suffer without blessing us.

In fact, as we continue to endure, He is preparing our table for us. But we must remain focused on what God has promised us and not look on our setbacks. We must not allow our trials to defeat the purpose of God in our lives. There will be times when God is taking us through our process and the spirits of loneliness and discouragement will sometimes make us feel like Elijah did in 1 Kings 19—that is, feeling as though we are the only one facing the situation.

But we should know that God is preparing millions for the End-Time harvest because there are still many who are lost. God is getting us ready to reap the harvest.

First Peter 5:6 shows us that God wants to exalt His people. But before He does, we have to go through a test so we won't steal His glory. We must keep in mind that God cannot fail, lie or make mistakes. As the song says, "His eye is on the sparrow." I know that at times we may feel as if we are less significant than a sparrow and wonder if He sees us in our suffering. Look up, child of God, and wonder no more, for He encourages us in the midst of our suffering.

We must continue to trust God in whatever state we find ourselves and remember that the grace of God will not lead us into a place where He cannot help us out. We must remember that He is the God of the valley and the God of the hills. He is still in control.

Let us look again at John the Baptist. John spent most of his life preparing for his ministry in the wilderness, and at his appearing, John was not lacking anything. He was bold, full of faith and power. He was ready to walk into the destiny that God had prepared for him.

We should never resist the things that God is doing in our lives. Even though everything does not to go our way, we must remember everything is working the way God planned it. Beloved, let us not be like a mule or a horse, but let us understand the will of God concerning us.

It is amazing how quickly we credit our setback in life to bad luck and our success to hard work.

As you read the Book of Esther, you find a remarkable assortment of setback and success. But one common thread runs through them all: God was at work behind the scene. He wove a beautiful lesson on sovereignty through the pages of her life, demonstrating that He was in control.

Be encouraged, for you will come out of your furnace of affliction: "But he knoweth the way that I take: when he hath tried me, I shall come forth as gold" (Job 23:10). That is what we are—gold. Let us welcome Him as He burns away the dross in our lives.

When we face the obstacles of this life, we sometimes look for a human savior to explain what God is doing in our lives, but we cannot expect someone else to understand what God is doing in our lives. We must seek to know the will of God in our lives. Even Jesus our Savior learned obedience through his suffering. (See Hebrews 5:8.)

Our feelings should not be mixed with the things we are facing at this moment, but must be in total submission to the will of God. We should come to a place of agreement with God and surrender our thoughts and feelings to Him. As we become more vulnerable to the will of God, we will understand why God puts us through these situations.

We are put in seclusion to learn how to deal with rejection, loneliness, misunderstandings and lies. These are the things that we sometimes face in our lives. We should not doubt the fact that even the thing that does hurt us is the very same thing that makes us. So we must understand that when God allows certain things in our lives to happen to us, it is because He is doing something dramatic in our lives, and we must not be moved.

Consider the beginning of David's life. For most of his life, David faced rejection. He was persecuted by his enemies, but it was all for his making as he became the greatest and most beloved king of Israel. Remember what he had to face to get to the top.

Sometimes for us to get to the top, God allows us to go through our own trials. Before we get to the glory, we must suffer. We've all heard the saying, *No pain no gain.* When God is getting ready to exalt us, we have to face things that we do not want to face, but we should be of good courage because John 16:33 says, "These things I have spoken unto you, that in me ye might have peace. In the world ye shall have tribulation; but be of good cheer; I have overcome the world."

So we see that even Jesus himself had to face the fact that in order for Him to minister effectively, He had to go through suffering. Hebrews 4:15 states, "For we have not an high priest which cannot be touched with the feeling of our infirmities; but was in all points tempted like as we are, yet without sin." There is something we should know before we face our trials: If we are not careful, the same trial that comes to make us strong can paralyze us and keep us in one place.

In Exodus 14, we are told that God hardened the heart of Pharaoh, King of Egypt, in order that He could receive the glory for miraculously delivering the

Israelites from slavery. At that point, the Israelites should have trusted God, but instead they allowed fear to grip and paralyze their lives so that they could not move. So God spoke to Moses to encourage the people to go forward.

There are some people who cannot go forward whenever they face trials because their worry, unbelief and/or disobedience bring about a heaviness. As believers, the only thing that should be unmovable is our faith in the Lord. We should remain steadfast, unmovable and always abounding in the work of the Lord.

As you and I know, it is impossible for us not to feel pain while we are in our wilderness. But we must continue to go forward, and we must keep on pushing. We should not let anything stop us from persevering. We must remember that we are the victor and not the victim.

In 2 Kings 6:13, Elisha and his servant were in the city called Dothan. As the enemy compassed the city, Elisha's servant was struck with fear. Elisha asked the Lord to open the eyes of his servant so that he could see in the spirit world. When his eyes were open spiritually, he saw chariots of fire surrounding them.

It is very easy for us to think that we are all alone when we are facing trials, but to the contrary, there is protection all around us.

As we walk through the wilderness, we cannot always understand the pathway on which we are traveling. The way may be rocky and rugged. We may fearfully travel along with uncertainty, loneliness and confusion lurking in the shadows. Our burdens may feel too heavy, and the annoyances all too common. We may sink in the marshlands or stumble and fall.

Oftentimes we cannot see the end of our trials or envision that the darkness of our night has a morning after it. But God promised that His presence shall go with us, and we can trust in His Word and unchanging love. He has promised to give us rest and a heart of calmness.

As we put our faith in Him, we may not understand the meaning of our trial until the storm passes over and the sun comes out. Then we will understand that the Master Artist weaves them together into a flawless perfection.

Every great and articulate servant of God must be broken before being used of God, because he or she cannot be puffed up and expect to be humble at the same time.

So we must become humble and broken before God.

Psalm 119:71, we see David confess, "It is good for me that I have been afflicted; that I might learn thy statutes." In Psalms 119:75, we see the sovereignty of God and the confession of David as he acknowledged, "I know, O LORD, that thy judgements are right, and that thou in faithfulness hast afflicted me."

Hold fast to what you know to be true:

- God will walk with you in your wilderness moments.
- God has a plan during your darkest moments.
- Your trial will last until God's plan is accomplished.

- Your sufferings will bring a deeper revelation of Jesus Christ.
- In your wilderness, you are being molded and shaped by God.
- What you learn in the wilderness, you will share with someone else.

Let us use Jesus as an example. Consider all the things to which He had to subject Himself. He experienced a life of persecution, suffering and pressure. Yet the Bible says that Jesus finished the race with joy. Let's look at how Jesus did it. Hebrews 12:2 reads, "Looking unto Jesus the author and finisher of our faith; who for the joy that was set before him endured the cross, despising the shame, and is set down at the right hand of the throne of God."

This scripture shows us clearly how Jesus did it. Jesus knew He had a destiny, but He had to go through obstacles in order to reach His goal. Thanks be to God! He did not despair in His sufferings as so many do. Jesus endured His suffering because He knew that through suffering, He would fulfill His purpose and make it to His destination. And He also knew that He would lead the way so that many others could follow. In staying His course, Jesus Christ has made an eternal impact. Hallelujah! Jesus could keep His composure because He knew what was happening to Him was preparing Him for something better; He knew where He was going.

We also notice that Jesus foresaw Himself coming out of His trials to the throne room of God. In fact,

Jesus did not keep His eyes on His shame and suffering. Instead, He kept His eyes on His victory. We should never look at ourselves and be discouraged about where we are, but rather we should look at and be encouraged about where we are going! That is why we are to walk by faith and not by sight. (See 2 Corinthians 5:7.)

Whenever we find ourselves in desperate situations, we should look to the Author and Finisher of our faith, and pattern ourselves after Him. Our trial is taking us to victory and not to defeat.

So I would encourage you as I encourage myself: *Let us not be like the children of Israel in the wilderness.*

In keeping their eyes on what they were experiencing, the children of Israel failed to see God's victory for their lives, and many of them failed to make it out of the wilderness alive. Let's not make the same mistake!

The children of Israel desired to make it to the land of Canaan without trusting God. Let us look at the land of Canaan. It was a land of a wealth—a land that God had promised to the children of Israel. But before they got to the land of Canaan, they had to go through the wilderness, a place where they first had to be proven before receiving the promise. Many did not receive the promise because they kept their eyes on the test and not on God. As a result, millions failed to make it out of the wilderness. It's sad that they kept looking at their circumstances and not holding the promise of God to be true. Beloved, we will always fail when we take our eyes off God's promises.

Our thoughts and mind should be consumed by God's promises. We should meditate on what God says and not on what we see. David the psalmist reminded God of His promises by saying "remember the promise which thou caused me to hope." David showed a determination to see God's promises fulfilled in his life in spite of his circumstances.

He was determined to see God's promises in action.

Let us look at the attitude of Jesus when the Holy Ghost led Him in the wilderness. (See Matthew 4.) Jesus was submissive to the Father's will. He demonstrated obedience, commitment and trust in God's Word. Note that Jesus escaped out of the wilderness without a snakebite because of trust. Jesus did not wander around like the children of Israel. Whenever we find ourselves wandering, we are not trusting God.

Whichever kind of wilderness we might find ourselves in, we must have an attentive ear, an attentive mind and a prayerful heart. Then we must expect for the Father to speak to us by dreams, visions, His word or His own voice to comfort us in our test. Let us remember the Hebrew words *Jehovah Shamar*, which mean "the God who is near" and not far.

Jesus also gives us assurance through His Word. We must note that the word *assurance* derives from the word *insurance*. It means a done deal. Titus 1:2 says, "In hope of eternal life, which God, that cannot lie, promised before the world began." There are things for which we must take responsibility, such as keeping a firm prayer life as we face the difficulties of this life.

Most believers faint when going through the storm and awake after the storm. We must stay awake in our trials and sleep after the storm. Romans 12:12 states, "rejoicing in hope, patient in tribulation, continuing instant in prayer." Prayer gives us a continuous strength to ride through the storm. The prophet Jonah said,

> When my soul fainted within me I remembered the LORD: and my prayer came in unto thee, into thine holy temple. They that observe lying vanities forsake their own mercy. But I will sacrifice unto thee with a voice of thanksgiving; I will pay that that I have vowed. Salvation is of the LORD.
> —JONAH 2:7–9

Jonah prayed from the fish's belly, God heard him, and the huge fish set him free by the direction and the power of God. When you pray, you are releasing words for help. The apostle James said, "The effectual fervent prayer of a righteous man availeth much" (James 5:16).

David the psalmist stated that a broken spirit and a contrite heart, God would not despise. Beloved, God will not shut out your prayer; you are defeated only when you stop praying.

Daniel sought God for change. While he was fasting and praying, there was a delay because there was a fight in the heavens. But Daniel never quit until he received an answer from the Lord! (See Daniel 19:12.)

Beloved, we should not give up when we cannot see

our way, because our darkest hour is just before change comes. Our answer is on the way! God will come into our prison, loose our shackles and set us free!

We must know that the blessing and the plan of God in our lives come with suffering. In fact, our sufferings move us closer to God's plan for our lives. Remember, God's plan for our lives is perfect, so His plans cannot be changed. God cannot be bribed or manipulated to change His perfect plan for our lives.

Sometimes, it seems hard to understand why those who love God seem to suffer the most. I believe that God has a far greater blessing for them; the sufferings will produce our blessings. Just like a traffic sign that alerts us to a stoplight ahead, suffering signals that our blessings are on the way.

Whenever we begin to feel uncomfortable, that means we are moving from our comfort zone into our blessings. We should note that the children of Israel were getting ready to enter into something new. But they hindered their own blessing by refusing to let go of what they had grown comfortable with in Egypt. Whenever they could not understand the new challenges they were facing, they complained.

Whenever we complain about something we cannot understand, like the children of Israel, we must remember that the earth is too small to contain God. He weighs the mountains in His hands, and the seas are like a drop of water in His hands. See how awesome He is! None are as mighty as He! None as intelligent as He! Let us trust the leading of His Spirit. Being born of the Spirit and filled with the Spirit is good, but we must also allow the Spirit to lead us. Abraham was led by the spirit of God from his father's land to a land of blessings. It is God's will for us to be blessed with unmerited success, but success can be dangerous without humility.

So while we patiently wait in our trials, there is evidence that God is right there with us:

He is keeping us alive.

His presence is in our lives.

He gives us instructions.

He shows us visions and dreams .

He encourages us through other people.

We must not allow the enemy to put the thought in our mind that God has brought us from sin to destroy us. We must know that there is a principle of God: When we trust God in our trials, we will see the hand of God in whatever we face. We must remember that when we become born again, we walk by faith. This means we are made with the capacity and capability to believe God for the impossible!

Each time we believe for the impossible, God's glory is revealed in our lives.There are things we must continue to believe for the glory of God. Yet, we must wait until they are manifested. It will sometimes seem impossible but keep on confessing what God said until it comes to pass.

We must know that God always puts us in situations where we must trust Him.

God will sometimes supply provision for us through the hands of others, but He also wants to bless us by our operating in our (God-given) ability to receive fresh manna for ourselves. I believe that God will, at times, take us from more than enough to just enough so that we can rely on Him. Whenever we face our wilderness, we must continue to press forward, and we must not be distracted.

We should always let the Lord encourage us as we travel our long and dusty road. We should never allow the journey to discourage us. We must never allow the things of this world to take the place of God in our lives. We must always remain firm in our trying times.

We must remember that the forces of darkness come to intimidate us, but in fact, they are intimidated by us because we have the armor of God—the belt of truth, the breastplate of righteousness, the shoes of the preparation of the gospel, the shield of faith, the helmet of salvation and the sword of the Spirit. (See Ephesians 6:14 −17.)

We sometimes may feel weak and out of it like Gideon (See Judges 6.), but we are a mighty men and women of valor. We are strong in the Lord! Gideon was a might man, but he thought that he was weak because of what he was facing. But the angel of the Lord appeared to him and addressed him as "mighty man of valour" (Judg. 6:12).

We must realize that God sometimes uses a drought in our lives to break us from pride. Also, the wilderness can be a place to make us become as a child that we might learn to walk in humility.

Let's look again at Joseph. In Genesis 37, we read about Joseph's prophetic dreams. Joseph may have never really comprehended it, but before he was able to fulfill God's purpose in his life, he had to go through several horrible situations. It began when his own brothers plotted against him and sold him into slavery. He spent about twelve years of his life in prison, getting ready for his destiny.

When the brothers confronted Joseph concerning what they did to him, Joseph only smiled with a joyous look on his face and replied, "you meant it for evil but God meant it for good." Sometimes the person we cannot stand is the one whom God is using to propel us into our destiny. We must know that God uses things, people, Satan (oh yes . . . Satan!) and the wilderness or whatever is necessary to get us to our destination.

So we see that the time that Joseph spent in prison was also in the plan of God so that he could be broken from everything that would stop him from being the leader that God would call him to be in Egypt. We must see our suffering as preparation. When we are fully prepared, God will launch us out into our destiny!

There are people who inherit or acquire certain positions of authority who, unfortunately, weren't broken before achieving such a position. Often, these people fail to excel in their position because they were not tested and broken prior to claiming their title. When leaders do not experience brokenness, self gets in the way of properly fulfilling their duty. They will most likely lack humility and abuse their authority. Many times a prideful leader's actions will lead to his own demise and negatively influence others.

Consider Peter and his walk with the Lord. To begin with, he was sincere but not broken. We read about some of Peter's mistakes in Matthew 16:22 when he rebuked the Lord, in John 18:10 when he used a sword to cut off the ear of Malchus and in Luke 22:54–62 when he denied the Lord three times.

After Peter denied the Lord, he realized what he had done, and the Bible says he "wept bitterly" (Luke 22:62). The fisherman—the rough, tough Peter—wept and eventually became humble. Everything he tried to do right somehow turned out wrong because he was not broken. He attempted to rely on his own strength and understanding. But after all his denial and the upper room experience, Peter became a true candidate for his position.

God desires to work on us and fix us before we fully inherit His promises.

The woman with the alabaster box also represents our lives. (See Luke 7:36, ff.) This incident exemplifies how precious and significant God ought to be in our lives. It shows us that if we do not get to the place of brokenness and humility, we can be of no use to God. We must be broken so that the sweet aroma that God has placed in us can flow out of our lives.

If we enter the wilderness as an angry person, we should come out a humble person. If we enter the wilderness without wisdom and knowledge, we should come out full of wisdom and knowledge. Regardless of how we enter our wilderness, we must return different. Our wilderness is designed to make us over again.

It is like the potter and the clay found in Jeremiah 18:2–6:

> The word which came to Jeremiah from the LORD, saying, Arise, and go down to the potter's house, and there I will cause thee to hear my words. Then I went down to the potter's house, and, behold he, wrought a work on the wheels. And the vessel that he made of clay was marred in the hand of the potter: so he made it again another vessel as seemed good to the potter to make it. Then the word of the LORD came to me, saying, O house of Israel, cannot I do with you as this potter? saith the LORD. Behold, as the clay is in the potter's hand, so are ye in mine hand, O house of Israel.

In this passage, God has given us a clear description of us in His hands. It's important to realize that just because we are in His hands, it does not necessarily mean that we are always in His will. We are in His will when we yield our will to His. His will for us is to make us into another vessel, but the Christians who are not willing to be made over will never grow into their full potential in God.

Many times, we do not like to spend time in solitude. A person who is willing to make time to spend alone in the presence of the Almighty God is more apt to allow the Lord to build his character and integrity. God wants us to be alone so that the Holy Ghost can reveal our true nature and rid us of selfishness, pride and any leaven that may be in our lives.

We must remember that the children of Israel were not sent out to the wilderness to be destroyed, but to be established. Oh, how often we think that our suffering comes to destroy us, but in fact, it comes to equip and prepare us. Let's look at it this way. Before we go on a journey, we make sure that the gas tank in our car is filled to get us to where we are going. Likewise, God fills us before the journey of our tests. Though it may not seem like it at times, I believe God grants us enough grace and supplies enough strength to go through our wilderness experiences. Let us be mindful of the apostle Paul when he wrote in 1 Corinthians 15:57, "Thanks be to God which give us the victory though our Lord Jesus Christ." God wants us to trust Him before He trusts us with His blessings. I believe there aren't too many believers whom God can really trust, particularly when they're under pressure and suffering. Many of us tend to drift away when pressure comes, but God intends for us to be steadfast and unmovable in Him.

We can see the steadfastness of Jesus as He agonized in prayer prior to His crucifixion. (See Luke 22:40, ff.) Even in His anguish and dread, He refused to quit praying. Just as Jesus looked unto the Father, we should also look to Him when we find ourselves in a place of anguish and dread.

Whenever we face the ups and downs of life and it seems like a roller coaster, we should stop, think and ask ourselves: *What would Jesus do in such a situation?*

Answer: *He would go for the ride until He reached His destination.*

Remember, your ups and downs will lead you to your destination.

God designs a place of testing for our lives, and His design is a simple plan for us—to come face to face with ourselves.

The last thing we want to confront is self. Being victorious over the devil and over the things of this world is good. But everyone's #1 enemy (this might come as a surprise to some and others may sharply disagree) is *himself*. Self had Judas betray and sell Jesus. Because of self, Peter denied Jesus. Because of self, Nimrod chose to build his own kingdom. Because of self, Nebuchadnezzar refused to take heed to the prophet of God and lost the kingdom of Babylon for seven years. Because of self, hell enlarges its mouth. Many people are plunging into the bottomless pit because of self's pride and arrogance.

Self is the last battle to win before we can win the victory. This is where the fight becomes intense because it is easier to be honest with others than with ourselves. We become best friends with this enemy. We sleep with it, eat with it, work with it and go to church with it. We carefully protect self. Therefore, self can only be confronted in the wilderness.

It was on Mount Moriah in Genesis 22 where Abraham proved to God that he was willing to put self aside and offer up his only son, Isaac. In return, a blessing was pronounced upon Abraham.

The trials in our wilderness are meant to kill self and

prompt us to reach for the blessings. There are those who would challenge what I say. Some Christians believe they should become successful overnight. But, if that were to happen, they would not love the Lord the same way. They may claim, "I will love the Lord the same way." Nevertheless, these same believers might automatically disqualify themselves by poor attendance of church services. If they can hardly make it to the church, how can they make a strong commitment if overnight success should come?

The description in Genesis 32 of Jacob wrestling with the angel shows us that nothing good comes easily. That is God's way of testing how badly we want God's blessing. If we are not willing to wrestle for what we want, we don't want it as bad as we think. Jacob wrestled with a supernatural being. Can you imagine what an awesome sight that must have been, seeing a man of flesh and blood wrestle with a celestial being? The Lord became so impressed with Jacob's determination to be blessed that his name was changed to Israel, which means "He who strives with God."

We can see two things that happen in this small narrative:

1. We see a promotion. Every struggle fought with determination leads to great promotion.
2. Jacob's name change represented a change in character, heart and spirit.

Whenever we find ourselves in a wilderness, it is because God wants to change our nature and character.

It is very important for us to be humble as we walk with the Lord. If we are not humble, we will not receive the blessings God has promised us. The reason our life seems to turn upside down after we receive a word of prophecy or knowledge of a promise is that our wilderness is a place where change, adjustment and humility take place. The wilderness is a place where we go through (perhaps painful) inconveniences in order for that promise to come alive in our life. It is a place where we become totally dependent on God in every area of our lives.

For the children of Israel, the wilderness also meant a place of deliverance. Keep in mind that they were guided into the wilderness after they were delivered from Egypt (Egypt representing physical bondage). As time went on, it seemed far more difficult for the Israelites to go through a deliverance that would get Egypt (mental and spiritual bondage) out of them. Deliverance was for their own good; it was for making them fit to receive the promises of God.

Like the Israelites, the Lord also wants to deliver us from sins that are locked into our hearts and bring those sins into the light.

God wants us to be delivered from self. It's just not good enough for us to come to the Lord; He also wants us to be delivered in our mind and in our emotions. Quoting the prophet Isaiah, Jesus said that He had come to "preach deliverance to the captives" (Lk. 4:18). The reason that many believers don't get along with those with whom they worship is that they come to God from Egypt, but they have not been delivered. So we can understand why there are so many people with crippled spirits and crippled emotions. They are out of Egypt, but there is no deliverance in their lives. Some are out of the habit of living in God's deliverance while others have the wrong attitude. Their minds are still in Egypt.

Romans 12:1–2 reminds us of the need for our minds to be changed. If our minds are not renewed, we cannot exercise our God-given ability to dominate the works of the devil. It is actually dangerous for a Christian to simply accept salvation yet possess a mind that is not transformed. The children of Israel were saved from Egypt, but their un-renewed minds kept them wandering in the desert. They were worried about onions and cucumbers ,contrary to what the Lord had told them before they went into the wilderness.

The Lord specifically told them that He was taking them to a land flowing with milk and honey. Beloved, if it were possible for them to get there without going through the wilderness, we can agree together that they would abuse the milk and honey because their minds were on onions and cucumbers.

God wants to deliver us from an Egyptian mentality and give us a heavenly mentality. Friend, there are times when we find ourselves in desperate situations—the same way we started out. We don't have what we used to have. It is as if you have been lowered into the valley of the shadow of death, robbed and stripped from what you once had. Even so, God has a raven to feed you.

God sometimes puts us in strange places, gives us just what we need and says nothing to us for weeks, months and years. You may be very astounded as you read that God would speak once and then remain silent for years. Well, consider Abraham and Sarah. They were promised by God to have a child; however, the promise took about twenty-five years to come to pass.

In those times of waiting for the promise of a child, we see that Sarah became weary. She told Abraham to have sexual relations with Haggar, and Haggar conceived and bore Ishmael.

We see in her time of waiting, Sarah was tempted to do her own thing. That sometimes happens to us as we wait on God's promises. Now, either we wait in our strange places, or we do our own thing. If we wait at the brook, God will have somebody to encourage and comfort us. And if He sees fit, He will even command our worst enemy to feed us.

God will provide for you a blessing, so that you, who had to beg, will be a blessing to thousands; because with man things are impossible, but with God all things are possible.

The Scriptures clearly tell us that "without faith, it is impossible to please [God]" (Heb. 11:6). So we should continue to believe God—even in our worst circumstance—for that which we believe will be possible.

In Mark 9:17–24, we read about a man who had a son possessed with a devil. The desperate man approached and began to explain to Jesus how he brought his son to the disciples and they could not cast the devil out of his son. Jesus then commanded that the son be brought to him. As they brought him, the Bible clearly states that the demonic spirit caused the son's condition to suddenly worsen. (See Mark 9:20.) We must remember that no matter how bad things get, it only happens because deliverance is near. When deliverance is near, things always seem to get worse. However, we must have faith in our darkest hour. Jesus said to the father of the son, "If thou canst believe, all things are possible to him that believeth."

The father then cried out "Lord, I believe; help thou mine unbelief." The father's reply was actually saying "Lord, I believe, but help me in whatever I may be doubting," and he received his victory. Whenever we are seeking God for things that seem difficult, we must constantly check every area in our lives to see if we have any unbelief. We should then confess it to God to clear it out of our way. Remember: *Without faith, it is impossible to please God.* And our desire should be to please God.

In Luke 1:28–38, even Mary received that for which she believed.

> And the angel came in unto her, and said, Hail, thou that art highly favoured, the Lord is with thee: blessed are thou among women. And when she saw him, she was troubled at his saying, and cast in her mind what manner of salutation this should be. And the angel said unto her, Fear not Mary: for thou hast found favour with God. And,

behold, thou shalt conceive in thy womb, and bring forth a son, and shalt call his name Jesus. He shall be great and shall be called the son of the Highest: and the Lord God shall give unto him the throne of his father David: and he shall reign over the house of Jacob forever; and of his kingdom there shall be no end. Then said Mary unto the angel, How shall this be, seeing that I know not a man? And the angel answered and said unto her, the Holy Ghost shall come upon thee, and the power of the Highest shall overshadow thee: therefore also that holy thing which shall be born of thee shall be called the Son of God and, behold, thy cousin Elizabeth, she had also conceived a son in her old age: and this is the sixth month with her, who was called barren. For with God nothing shall be impossible. And Mary said, Behold the handmaid of the Lord; be it unto me according to thy word. And the angel departed from her.

Also verse 45 shows us her victory and her faith: "And blessed is she that believed: for there shall be a performance of those things which were told her from the Lord."

Our wilderness is a preparation for the things God is going to do with us. After every word from the Lord, there is always opposition. However, if you keep believing, there will be a performance of what God says. Because Mary believed and trusted in something that looked impossible, God accomplished His work in and through her.

Beloved, let us continue to believe, because there were millions who died in the wilderness because of doubt. Hebrews 3:18–19 states that "And to whom sware he that they should not enter into his rest, but to them that believe not? So we see that they could not enter in because of unbelief."

Yet Joshua and Caleb were victorious in the wilderness because of their faith.

Hebrews 4:3 declares that "we which have believed do enter into rest." Beloved, your faith is giving you rest until you receive your blessing.

It is very important that we try our very best to keep a good attitude while we are in our wilderness because our attitude can determine our altitude in victory and in God. In the wilderness, those who had an attitude of faith were always spared from snakebite, earthquake and every other disaster. If our attitude is not full of faith, it can lead us to complain. And complaining brought the wrath of God out on those who were in the wilderness. Even Aaron and Miriam, who complained about Moses' wife in Numbers 12, were called out of the congregation, and God came down in a cloud and reprimanded them. Miriam was made leprous.

You might not be complaining with your mouth, but you might be complaining in the temple of your heart. In Numbers 17, we read that the Lord told Moses, "Bring Aaron's rod again before the testimony, to be kept for a token against the rebels; and thou shalt quite take away their murmurings from me, that they die not" (Num. 17:10).

Perhaps you are prone to complain about your financial difficulties. If so, the Bible provides us illustrations of how to get out of a "financial wilderness" through *giving!* In Acts chapter 10, Cornelius was in need, and the Lord heard his prayer and also saw his giving. As a result of his giving, the Lord sent the help he needed.

Also in Mark 8:2–9, the Bible speaks of a boy with five loaves and two fishes who gave his lunch to feed four thousand people, not considering his three-day journey back home without food. Furthermore, I believe the seven baskets that were left over were given back to him because the lad gave his last. Jesus said, "Give and it shall be given unto you; good measure, pressed down, and shaken together, and running over, shall man give into your bosom" (Lk. 6:38).

We at the Greater Anointing Harvest Church have been experiencing a transition from a financial wilderness to a place of blessing. It started to happen as I began to teach and preach on the topic, "God Wants to See Your Faith." If you recall, Jesus often asked His disciples, "Where is your faith?" Along with that teaching, there were people in the church, including my wife and me, whose hearts were touched to make financial vows unto God and to prove Him.

Second Corinthians 9 gives us the answer for coming out of our financial wilderness. The Macedonian church, the poorest church throughout the New Testament churches mentioned in the Bible, became very wealthy. Imagine, from rags to riches. How was it possible? Simple. Learn to give without fear because giving with fear shows that we are not trusting God.

When we give, trusting God's Word, He will return it back to us with increase. The Macedonian church gave their way out of their financial wilderness. They turned their situation around by giving out of their needs. With the amount of money my wife and I gave sacrificially, we could have purchased two better cars than what we were driving. However, we believed that if we were to give the biggest and best offering to God first, He would give us His best in return.

Several months after our time of sacrificial giving, my wife received a car that she was once only able to dream about. But the dream became a reality. I believe that because we gave out of our needs, God multiplied it back to us double. Since we found the Macedonian church's remedy to their financial wilderness was giving their best to God, we tried it also. There have been scores of testimonies from those who were bold enough to believe and try Him.

I encourage those of you who are in a financial wilderness. Instead of complaining and worrying, give the best that you can and keep on giving. Yes, you will be tried and tested in your giving, but always remember what God has promised: "Prove me now herewith, saith the LORD of hosts, if I will not open you the windows of heaven, and pour you out a blessing, that there shall not be room enough to receive it" (Mal. 3:10).

The Bible records an interesting story about a woman from Zarephath in 1 Kings:

And the word of the Lord came unto [Elijah], saying, Arise, get thee to Zarephath, which belongeth to Zidon, and dwell there: Behold, I have commanded a widow woman there to sustain thee.

So he arose and went to Zarephath. And when he came to the gate of the city, behold, the widow woman was there gathering of sticks: and he called to her, and said, Fetch me, I pray thee, a little water in a vessel, that I may drink. And as she was going to fetch it, he called to her, and said, Bring me, I pray thee, a morsel of bread in thine hand.

And she said, As the LORD thy God liveth, I have not a cake, but an handful of meal in a barrel, and a little oil in a cruse: and, behold, I am gathering two sticks, that I may go in and dress it for me and my son, that we may eat it, and die. And Elijah said unto her, Fear not; go and do as thou hast said: but make thereof a little cake first, and bring it unto me, and after make for thee and for thy son.

For thus saith the LORD God of Israel, The barrel of meal shall not waste, neither shall the cruse of oil fail, until the day that the LORD sendeth rain upon the earth. And she went and did according to the saying of Elijah: and she, and he, and her house, did eat many days. And the barrel of meal wasted not, neither did the cruse of oil fail, according to the word of the LORD, which he spake by Elijah.

—1 KINGS 17:8–16

In Luke 21:1–4, we read about another woman who gave all she had to the work of God. This woman's faith moved the heart of Jesus, and He used her giving as an example for us. We, too, can move the heart of God by our giving, despite whatever financial wilderness we find ourselves in.

While waiting on the Lord in difficulties we should not rely on our own understanding. Instead we should give God our total obedience. We know that when we walk through the valley of the shadow of death, we should fear no evil, for He is with us. God is with us in whatever wilderness we find ourselves.

Therefore, do not fear . . . just *believe*!

Believe that you shall find, not only survive your wilderness experience, but you shall emerge victorious, ready to fulfill God's perfect plan for your life!

TO CONTACT THE AUTHOR:

Pastor A. J. Beech
P.O. Box 256072
Dorchester, MA 02125
Phone: (617) 333-1144
Email: ajb-book@hotmail.com